I0004747

# A n00b's Guide to Using Autodesk Maya 2(

By Gregory Marlow

**Tech N00b Books**

www.techn00b.com

# Table of Contents

# Introduction: What is Autodesk Maya?

A seemingly infinite number of software packages on the market are competing for your attention and hard earned dollars. So it is always a good idea to ask: What is this program, and what can it do for me? When asking those questions about Autodesk Maya, be prepared for a long answer.

Maya is a powerful 3D asset creation package capable of high-end modeling, texturing, rigging, animation, lighting, rendering, compositing, and dynamic simulation. It has been used for creative projects ranging from animated feature films to AAA video games; from medical simulations to print advertisements; from children's book illustrations to educational and training software.

Maya is a versatile tool that thousands of creative people have bent to their will in order to achieve innovative solutions to complex problems. But in all its versatile glory, Maya is only as good as the driver behind the wheel. So buckle up.

# Chapter 1: Maya's Interface

## *3D and the Cartesian Coordinate System*

It seems that we are constantly bombarded with the term "3D." As you may already know, 3D is short for three-dimensional, and it refers to the three spatial dimensions that make up the world around us. If you stand up and walk around the room, you will see that you can move left and right, up and down, forward and backward. These are the three spatial dimensions. It is difficult to even imagine a universe without one of them.

Yet we all use one and two dimensional concepts every day. Let's start with the first dimension. If someone asks you to cut a piece of string to a certain length, the person might say, "Cut it three inches long." With this single dimension, you have all the information needed. You know where the string begins, and now all you have to do is measure three inches in a single dimension to know exactly where to cut. Communicating any point on a single dimension only requires an origin (starting point) and a single dimension, in this case, three inches.

However, when you bring the second dimension into play, the concept is more complicated. If someone asks you to draw a dot at a specific location on a piece of paper, a single dimension isn't enough information. You would need an instruction like "Three inches over, and four inches up." A point in two-dimensional space requires two numbers. The Cartesian coordinate system generally labels the two dimensions as X (horizontal) and Y (vertical). Using this system, you can communicate any point on a 2D plane with two numbers written like this: (X,Y). As long as you know the origin (0,0) and the coordinate, you can define any point in 2D space. A coordinate such as (4,3) would tell you that the point is four units along the horizontal X axis and three units up the vertical Y axis.

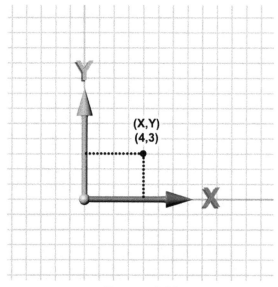

*Figure: 1.01*

Likewise, when the third dimension enters the picture, you can define any point in 3D space with three coordinates, X, Y, and Z, as long as you know the origin point. It is important to note that the origin point is where all three of these axes meet. If you know the location of (0,0,0) then you can find any other point in space, such as (5,5,3).

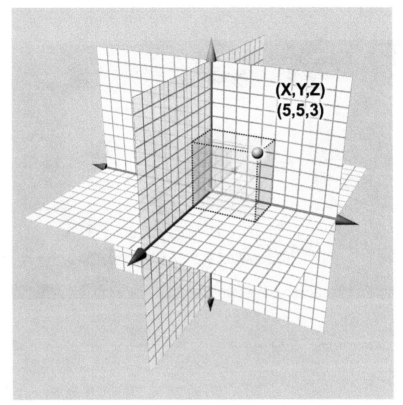

Figure: 1.02

Maya and almost every other 3D package uses this Cartesian coordinate system to define 3D space. They will usually indicate the three axes with the RGB color system. X is red, Y is green, and Z is blue. This serves as a helpful little reminder for art-minded users.

## Maya's User Interface

The first time you open Maya you may feel a bit intimidated with what you see. Nearly every inch of the interface is packed with cryptic icons and menus containing mysterious terms, like "subdivs." It is hard to not feel overwhelmed. But realize Maya is a tool for many different types of users. Many of the things that make the interface feel complicated are actually redundant ways of doing the same thing. For example, if you want to create a sphere, the interface has at least six ways to do it. Maya's interface is complicated in order to accommodate itself to every possible workflow option a user might prefer.

In the process of learning to use Maya, questions will obviously arise. F1 is the shortcut key to activate Maya's documentation and help material. F1 is used across many programs as the shortcut key for *Help*, but with the diverse and numerous options in Maya, it can be a refuge for both beginners and old pros alike.

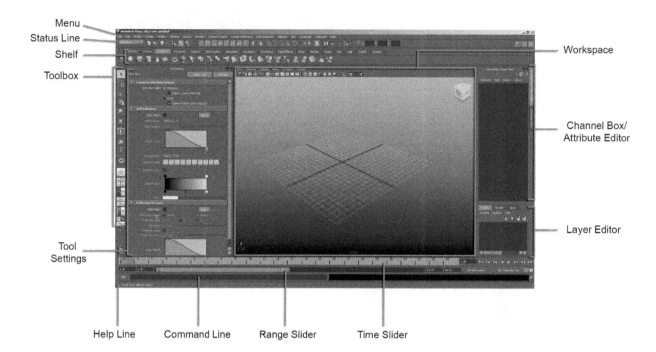

Menu
Status Line
Shelf
Toolbox

Tool
Settings

Workspace

Channel Box/
Attribute Editor

Layer Editor

Help Line    Command Line    Range Slider    Time Slider

*Figure: 1.03*

**Main Menu**

No matter how hard some programs try to avoid it, a good old-fashioned menu possesses an elegant simplicity. So let's start there. First, turn on all the different UI elements by choosing *Display>UI Elements>Show All UI Elements*. (Tip: the ">" symbol will indicate moving to the next step.) Your screen will possibly be more crowded, but it should look like the image in Figure: 1.03

Maya's menu should seem very familiar with the standard *File* and *Help* options. But despite its simple appearance, it is quite powerful. Nearly every tool, option, preference, and setting in Maya can be found in the menu, just not all at the same time. The volume of content creation tools that Maya contains is massive. The UI simplifies the organization of all these menu items with the status line.

**Status Line**

The status line is the icon-filled toolbar directly below the menu. The first item on the status line is a drop-down box called the *Menu set menu* (yes, that is really its name). The *Menu set menu* allows you to switch between the different categories of menus. If clicked, the *Menu set menu* expands into a list of the general categories Maya uses to organize its many tools. These menu sets are *Animation, Polygons, Surfaces*, *Dynamics*, *Rendering*, *nDynamics*, and *Customize*.

When the different categories are selected, the items on the main menu, above the status line, will change to accommodate that category. The first seven menu items stay the same in all the different menu sets, and the *Help* menu is always the last menu item. The rest of the menu changes to offer category-specific options. If you are in the *Animation* menu set, you will see options like *Animate*, *Create Deformers*, and *Skeleton*. If you are in the *Polygons* set, you will see options like *Mesh*,

*Normals*, and *Create UV's*. The purpose of these sets is to group together the tools you might need when in a specific stage of production.

Of course, sometimes you will find yourself needing a tool from a different menu as you work. For example, the deformers are often handy modeling tools. You can click between different menu sets or you can change the menu sets using the shortcut keys: F2, F3, F4, F5, and F6.

Keeping with Maya's propensity for customization, you can also create your own custom menu set by selecting *Customize* from the drop-down menu.

### Shelf

Some people are more visual and are not fond of digging through drop down boxes to find what they want. The shelf accommodates those users. The shelf is the series of labeled tabs directly below the status line. If you click on the tabs, you will see that the icons in the shelf change. Unlike the menu, the shelf is not a complete list of everything you can do in Maya. Rather it is a grouping of commonly used tasks in each of the categories. However, the shelf does offer one major advantage to the menu: it is extremely customizable. It is very simple to create your own button for the shelf that will perform very complicated tasks in a single click.

### Tool Box

Along the side of your screen, you will see a thin row of vertical icons. This section is called your toolbox. It is divided into two sections with a small gap between the icons, about halfway down. The top half contains the basic selection and manipulation tools. The bottom half are quick layout buttons for different workspace layouts.

### Tool Settings

The area to the immediate right of the toolbox is the tool settings window. If you click through the different tools in this top half of the toolbox, you will notice that the content of the tool settings window changes. Tools settings allow you to change the options for the tool you have selected for use.

### Channel Box/Attribute Editor/Layer Editor

When you create an object in Maya, it has many attributes. All of these attributes can be found, edited, and organized in the area along the right side of the user interface. Two vertical tabs along the right edge of the user interface allow you to switch between the *Channel Box/Layer Editor* and the *Attribute Editor*. All of these will be empty at this time, but once you actually have objects selected these editors will fill up with a lot of useful information.

The channel box is a quick and clean way of making alterations to select editable options. This is also where you will be able to see the nodes that make up the construction history of an object. A node is a single element of the computational data that makes up everything inside of Maya. These nodes are connected together to form more complex graphs. Behind every element in Maya is one of these complex node graphs.

The layer editor is Maya's way of allowing you to group the objects for organization. There are many different types of "grouping" in Maya. The layer editor is for organizational purposes only.

The attribute editor is where all the attributes pertaining to your object and its nodes are stored and can be changed. The amount of data you will find in the attribute editor is daunting. But think of it as the nuts and bolts of how your object is constructed. It often requires a bit of digging to find the exact attribute you might need to edit, but fortunately most of the attributes you will be using are represented in the channel box.

### Time Slider

The time slider is the numbered line that goes across the bottom of the screen. Although it has far more functionality, it is similar in operation to a video time line on Quicktime, Windows Media Player, or Youtube. The numbers represent "frames" rather than seconds, and the playback buttons on the far right of the time slider have a few animation-specific options. You can click and drag along the slider to change the current frame. Notice that if you type a number into the input box to the immediate right of the time slider the current frame changes to that number.

### Range Slider

The range slider allows you to specify the length of the time line in the time slider. One second of film animation is 24 frames or 30 frames for games and television. So if you need to do a film animation that is ten seconds long, you need 240 frames. In this example, you would use the outer-most input boxes to set the animation range of 1 and 240. While the innermost input boxes set your playback range, the part of the animation that you wish to show is on the time slider. You can manually adjust the playback range by clicking and dragging on the boxes at either end of the range slider bar.

### Command Line

Every action you perform in Maya executes a command. For example, if you move an object one unit in the X axis, the command that is executed is: move -r 1 0 0. These commands will not be your primary way of performing specific actions in Maya, especially early in your usage. But these commands can be very powerful. We will learn how to harness some of their power later, but for now just note that when you perform a task in Maya, like creating or moving an object, the command for that action will print on the right side of the command line. If you copy and paste that same command into the left side of the command line, the action will be repeated.

### Help Line

The cryptic icons in Maya's user interface are sometimes hard to decipher for a newcomer and sometimes even for a long-time user. To help with this, Maya has the help line. The help line is the thin gray bar that extends across the very bottom of the UI. If you mouse over an icon or menu item, a short explanation of the tool will be shown in the help line. You will also see these tips when mousing over many different items in Maya's UI. Sometimes it will also provide additional information for using the tool you have selected.

**Workspace**

The workspace is in the center of Maya's user interface. This is where you will spend the bulk of your time in Maya. By default you will see an empty area with a grid. This is your perspective camera view. You are literally looking through the eye of a virtual camera into the three-dimensional world in which you will be creating objects.

Along the top of the workspace is the panel menu and panel toolbar that allow you to change many of the workspace settings.

## *Working in the Workspace*

An empty scene is boring, so let's create something for you to see inside of your workspace. First, in the main menu, make sure *Create>Polygon Primitives>Interactive Creation* is unchecked. This will create new objects at the origin point (0,0,0). Now click on *Create>Polygon Primitives>Sphere*. You should now see a sphere at the center of the grid in your workspace.

The workspace is where you will create and manipulate the items in your scene. At this time, the sphere is most likely displaying in the view as a blue wire mesh. You can change the way the mesh displays in the workspace. Press 4 to display wire frame, 5 to display smooth shaded, 6 to display texture (if a texture map is applied to the model), and 7 to display the preview lighting. Additional display modes are available in the panel menu, at the top of the workspace, under *Shading*. For this exercise, press 5 for smooth shaded.

The default workspace layout is a single perspective camera view. Change this by selecting the second quick layout button with the icon of four split panels shown in Figure: 1.04. You should see four different camera views with the top right panel being a perspective view. The other three panels should be a top, side, and front orthographic view. Objects appear flat in an orthographic view. In a perspective view, an object's apparent size changes depending on its distance from the camera. Distant objects seem smaller and near objects appear larger. Our eyes see in perspective. But in an orthographic view, objects are the same size no matter how close or far away from the camera they may

*Figure: 1.04*

be. This allows you to obtain an objective view of an object's shape and form from a single angle wi thout distorted foreshortening effects.

The four panel layout is often used so you can see an object from multiple angles at once. But if you mouse over one of the views and tap the space bar, that view will be maximized. Tapping the space bar again will return you to the four-paneled view.

The perspective view is a virtual camera. You are literally looking through the eye of a camera at a virtual 3D world. So think of navigating around the scene as moving a video camera.

Maya gives you three view navigational options: tumble, track, and dolly. To tumble hold down the alt key and left click drag in the perspective view. Tumbling allows you to orbit around the focal point of your camera. If you have an object selected, you can change that object's focal point by tapping your "F" key. If nothing is selected, Maya will focus on the entire content of the scene.

To track hold down the alt key and the middle mouse button, then drag in the perspective view. Tracking moves your camera and the camera's focal point side to side and up and down.

To dolly hold down alt and the right mouse button and drag in the perspective view. Dollying is often confused with zooming, but although the effects seem similar, they are not the same. When you zoom on a camera, you are changing the lens length but the camera never moves. The changing of the lens length creates a telescopic effect and often causes distortion and exaggerated shapes. When you dolly the camera, you are physically moving the camera closer or further away from the focal point. Dollying is as if you were walking to and fro with the camera. Zooming is as if you were standing still and letting the camera do the work with the lens.

A light gray box called the view cube is in the top right corner of the perspective view. By clicking on the cube and dragging, you can tumble. By selecting the different faces and edges of the cube, your camera orients to preset angles. The house-shaped button or home key at the top left corner of the view cube returns the camera to the default camera perspective.

You will find that you are able to track and dolly in an orthographic view the same as you did in perspective. However, the camera is locked in one angle, disabling your ability to tumble. If you select the view cube and drag, you will be able to tumble the orthographic camera. It is important to note that this camera is still orthographic; it is just no longer locked in the side angle. The lack of foreshortening on the grid is evidence of this.

Let's return to the perspective view and explore selecting and transforming objects. In the toolbox, choose the top button with the "pointer" icon. This is the select tool. You can also activate the select tool by pressing your "Q" key. You can now click on the sphere in the workspace to select it. The sphere's wire frame will highlight green when it is selected.

You can marquee select multiple items. Holding shift allows you to toggle add and remove items from your selection. Holding Ctrl removes items from the selection, while holding Shift+Ctrl allows you to add to the selection.

The shortcut key to move an object is "W." The move tool can also be found in the tool box. It is the fourth icon down with a picture of an arrow and a cone. Once you have activated the move tool you will see a red, green, and blue arrow each pointing in a different direction; this is the translate manipulator. These three arrows coincide with the Cartesian coordinate system's X,Y, and Z axes. Again, X is red, Y is green, and Z is blue. It is also notable that a tiny XYZ axis reference in the bottom left corner of the perspective view shows you the world orientation.

After you have activated the move tool, you can select an axis and drag the object along that axis to move it. If you select the yellow square in the center of the translate manipulator, you can move the object in multiple axes at once, although you will be moving the object relative to your camera's angle of view.

If you open the channel box while moving the object, you will see that the translate X, Y, and Z values update in real time. You can also type in values in each of the channels and the sphere will move accordingly. Select the *Translate X* channel by clicking on the text. Now if you middle mouse drag in the workspace, the value will update. You can adjust more than one channel at one time by holding Ctrl while you select the channels, or by click-dragging to highlight multiple channels.

The shortcut key to activate the rotate tool is "E" and the scale tool is "R." Each allows you to change the rotation and scale of the sphere one axis at a time or all three axes together. Rotation and scale can also be edited in the channel box. Take note that the numbers in translate, rotate, and scale each represent a different thing. Typing 45 in Translate X will move the ball 45 units in the X axis; typing 45 in Rotate X will rotate the ball 45 degrees around the X axis, and typing 45 into Scale X will scale the ball to 45 times its creation size in the X axis.

## *Hotbox and Marking Menus*

Maya has yet another way to access menu options. If you press and hold the space bar, a menu will pop up around your mouse pointer. This is the hotbox. It contains a massive amount of options and many users like this option because it requires less mouse movement to find your needed options, and it increases the speed of work flow.

If you click in the center of the hotbox on the word *Maya,* you open a camera selection marking menu. Marking menus allow you to make selections by using directional marks with the mouse rather than clicking. Maya has many marking menus to help users work more efficiently on repetitive processes.

This brief introduction to Maya's awesome UI design should be used as a reference as you work through the exercises in this book and on personal projects. Although complex, the many options and tabs are really designed to increase speed and production while you develop your own personal work flow. Remember, the best way to learn what a function does is to try it.

# Chapter 2: Modeling

Modeling is the creation and manipulation of 3D geometry. In this chapter, we are going to discuss two different types of geometry you can create in Maya: *NURBS* and *Polygons*. Each of these model types refer to mathematical ways of representing a surface in 3D space. NURBS and Polygons differ in many ways but they both output a render-able geometry, and they are both made up of editable construction elements. At the level of the object (also called "in object mode"), we can translate, rotate, and scale both types of geometry. But short of stacking primitive shapes together, your modeling power is somewhat limited with these tools. To actually make unique, detailed models, we will need to be able to make alterations on the "sub-object" level. NURBS and Polygon geometry are made up of different types of sub-objects. Let's explore each of them individually.

## *NURBS*

URBS is an acronym for Non-Uniform Rational B-Spline. A B-spline is a curve that is defined by a small amount of control points. Let's create a spline by going to *Create>CV Curve Tool*. In the side view, click six times in random places to create the control points, then press enter. You will see that you now have a smooth curve that uses the six points you defined as guides for its shape. If you right click on the curve, a marking menu will pop up around your mouse pointer. Drag your mouse over *Control Vertex*, and release the mouse button to select it. You are now able to adjust the original points

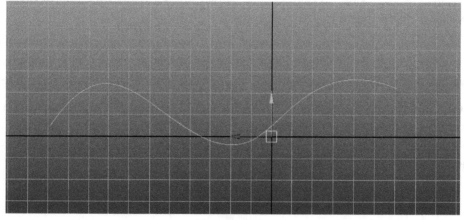

*Figure: 2.01*

you created to alter the shape of the curve. When doing this, you are editing the curve on the sub-object level. Right click on the curve again, and choose *Object* to return back to the object level.

Now create a second curve of a different shape in the side view containing six points, and move it forward in the X axis as seen in Figure: 2.02. Hold shift to toggle select both curves, and under the

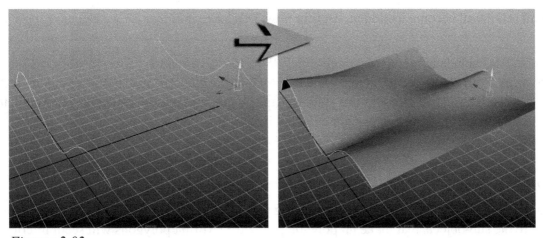

*Figure: 2.02*

surfaces menu set, click *Surfaces>Loft*.

You now have a surface with edges defined by the two curves you created. Select one of the curves and move it; you will see that the surface updates in real time. If you right click on one of the creation curves and edit the control vertices on the sub-object level, the surface will update, too. Maya retains the history information on how the surface was created and allows you to use that construction history to continue to edit the object. If you select the lofted surface and go to *Edit>Delete by Type>History,* the construction history will be deleted and editing the original curves will not update the surface anymore. But the surface itself also has a sub-object level where you can edit the control points to

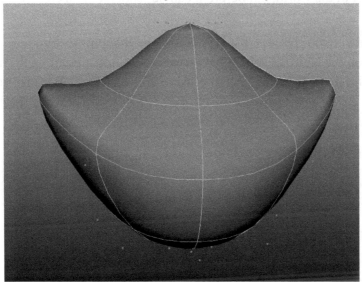

*Figure: 2.03*

adjust the shape of the model. You enter the surface's sub-object level the same way as you did for the curve, by right clicking on the object and choosing the sub-object you wish to edit. We will learn about more of these sub-objects later, but for now the *Control Vertex* and the *Hull* sub-object types will allow you to make quick adjustments to the surface's shape.

Let's hide our NURBS surface and curves by selecting them and pressing Ctrl+H. The objects still exist in your scene, they are just hidden. To see all the objects that are hidden and visible in your scene, go to *Window>Outliner*. The outliner is a complete hierarchical list of every object in your scene. Selecting an object in the outliner also selects it in your scene. If you select *loftedSurface1* and press Shift+H, it will become unhidden. But for now, let's leave it hidden so we can have more room to work.

Create a NURBS sphere by going to *Create>NURBS Primitives>Sphere*. This sphere is made out of NURBS surfaces all connected together. Note that each of the NURBS surfaces or "patches" is defined by a curve as well. You can also edit this sphere shape by going to the sub-object level. Again, to access the sub-object marking menu, right click on the object.

## *Polygons*

Create a polygon primitive sphere again by clicking on *Create>Polygon Primitives>Sphere*. Now we can explore the sub-objects that make up polygon geometry. At first polygons will seem inferior to NURBS due to the distinct blocky, faceted appearance of the model. The edges in a polygon model are made up of rigid, straight lines unlike the smooth NURBS curves. So you may be surprised to hear that most professional modelers prefer polygon modeling to NURBS modeling, even when creating organic, smooth meshes.

Polygon modeling, sometimes referred to as box modeling, is popular because polygons are exceedingly versatile and easy to manipulate. An efficiently modeled polygon object also requires less math to calculate than a NURBS model. Video game models are made of polygons because graphics processors (GPU's) are designed to only render polygon objects, not NURBS. So you can create the greatest NURBS model in the world, but before it can be rendered, it is converted to polygons by your GPU.

Perhaps the biggest "pro" in our pro/con list is polygon's predictability. You may have noticed, when editing control points on the NURBS sphere, you were not editing a point on the surface of the sphere. You were editing a point that only influenced the shape of the surface. Because you are indirectly

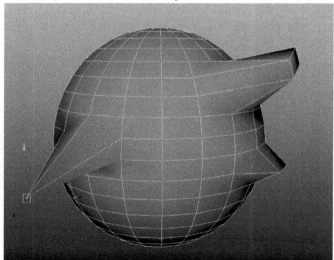

*Figure: 2.04*

changing the shape of the NURBS surfaces the results are often unpredictable. When modeling in polygons, all of your edits are made to the actual surface of model.

The only unpredictability issue that comes with polygon modeling is when you decide to smooth the object. Smoothing a polygon object is rounding its sharp edges by increasing its number of polygons.

However, if the model has an appropriate amount of fidelity, smoothing is still very predictable.

Let's explore the different polygon sub-objects by right clicking on the polygon sphere. The marking menu that comes up has many options but the three primary sub-object types we are going to focus on are *Vertex*, *Edge*, and *Face*.

Select *Vertex*, *Edge* and *Face* in turn, and manipulate the sub-objects to see how they affect the mesh. A vertex is a point on the surface of the polygon model. An edge is a straight line that connects any two vertices (plural of vertex). A face is an area enclosed by edges.

You can manipulate each of these with the translate, rotate, and scale tools to directly change the shape of the model. Notice that the rotate and scale tools have no real effect if used on a single vertex, but if several vertices are selected, you can make adjustments to the shape of the object very quickly.

It is important to note that a face can be an area enclosed by three polygons or a thousand. But for efficiency and control, standard practices in modeling are to keep faces four-sided (quads) or three-sided (triangles). It is also noteworthy to mention that a quad is simply two triangles with a shared invisible edge

Keep these concepts in your mind when working with these sub-objects. It will help you visualize the shapes and forms you wish to create.

Now we have the base understanding of the sub-object editing options for NURBS and polygon geometry. Let's put that knowledge to work by actually creating a model of something you would find

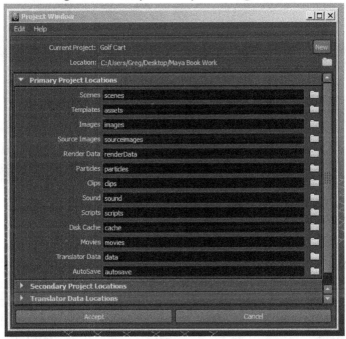

*Figure: 2.05*

in the real world. Along the way, we will also learn some new tools to create, refine, and edit your models.

## *Modeling a Golf Cart*

Setting up the scene

For your first modeling project, you are going to create a golf cart. But first, Maya is going to need to know where to save all of the related files that go along with every Maya project, such as texture maps, rendered images, and save files. To keep all of these files together Maya allows you to create and assign project folders.

A project folder is created by clicking *File>Project Window*. The window that will open will look like Figure: 2.05. Name the project "Golf Cart," and set the location to a work folder of your choosing. You will see a long list of folder names under the primary project locations tab. These are the default folders Maya will create under the Golf Cart folder to store your work files. Click *Accept* to create the project folder.

After you have created the project, make sure Maya is associating your files with the project you just created by going to *File>Set Project*. Choose the *Golf Cart* folder, and click *set*. *Set Project Folder* allows you to switch back and forth between the different projects you may be working on at one time.

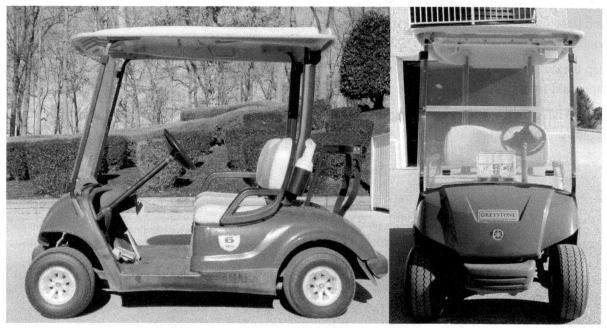

*Figure: 2.06*

Let's start with a fresh new file by going to *File>New Scene*.

Creating a customized workspace layout will allow you to quickly change between the different views you need to model this golf cart. Along the top of the workspace, you will see the words: *View, Shading, Lighting, Show, Renderer, and Panel*. This is the panel menu. From the panel menu select *Panels>Layouts> Three Panes Split Left*. This will divide your workspace into three panels, two small panels on the left and one tall panel on the right. We want the two left panels to be the orthographic front and side views while the right will be the perspective view. In the top left panel, go to *Panels>Orthographic >Front*; on the lower left Panel, go to *Panels>Orthographic>Side*, and on the right panel, go to *Panels >Perspective>persp*.

Before starting any model, or any art project at all for that matter, it is best to gather as much reference material as possible. Below you will find a front and a side view of a golf cart. We will take these images into Maya to help get the correct placement and general shape of the objects. For this example, use the reference as suggestion, not an exact blueprint. Feel free to experiment along the way.

We want to be able to see the front image of the golf cart in the front view and the side image in the side view. To do this, we are going to create an image plane for each of the two orthographic views. In the front view panel menu, choose *View>Select Camera*. If your attribute editor is not open, select the *Attribute Editor* tab along the right edge of the screen to open it. In the attribute editor, you should see the attributes for the front camera you selected. Along the top of the attribute editor, you will see the words *front* and *frontShape*. These are the nodes that make up the front camera. The node that we are going to look at is *frontShape*. You will find a long list of attribute categories in expandable tabs with names like *Camera Attributes*, *Film Back*, and *Depth of Field*. Scroll down till you find the *Environment* tab and click on the tiny triangle to expand it. Click on the large *Create* button in the *Image Plane* attribute.

You will notice that the node tab along the top now says *imagePlane1*. That is because you have created another node in the graph as an input for the *frontShape* node. A simplified way of understanding this is to say that the *imagePlane1* node is feeding information to the *frontShape* node.

Under the *imagePlane1* node, you will find the *Image Name* attribute. This will allow you to point to an image in your project folder to place on the image plane. But at this time you don't have any images in your project folder. The reference images can be found online at: <http://flic.kr/s/aHsjz7dEA8>. Save the images to the *source images* folder in your Maya project.

Now when you select the folder icon in the *Image Name* attribute, you can navigate to the source images, and select the *Front.jpg* file, and hit open. In your perspective and front views, you should be able to see the image of the golf cart.

Let's adjust the placement of the image plane so the golf cart is centered and the tires line up along the grid. Also, we will want to scoot the image plane along the Z axis, so it will still be visible in the front view but won't be in our way in the perspective and side views. In the *imagePlane1* node under the *Placement Extras* tab, we are going to change the *Center* coordinates. Although not labeled, the three

Figure: 2.07

coordinates are in XYZ order. Change the current center coordinates to 0.3, 10.3, and -50.

Now, you are going to create an image plane in the side view to display the side image of the golf cart. Let's mix it up, and do it a different way this time. On the side view panel menu, choose *View>Image Plane>Import Image*. Choose *Side.jpg*, and hit *Open*. You now have the side image plane, *imagePlane2*, visible in the three views.

Again, you are going to place the center of this image plane as we did in the side view. Select the side view camera by choosing *View>Select Camera* in the panel menu. This time we will edit it in the channel box. Again, you can switch between the channel box and attribute editor by selecting the side tabs on the far right of the screen. At the bottom of the attribute editor, you will see the word *INPUTS* with *imagePlane2* below it. Click on *imagePlane2* to expand it in the channel box. Enter -50 for Center X, 10.3 for Center Y, and 0 for Center Z.

Now the image planes are in place displaying the reference images. Your scene should look something like Figure: 2.07.

## Polygon modeling

You are ready to start creating the geometry of the golf cart. However, sometimes it is hard to know

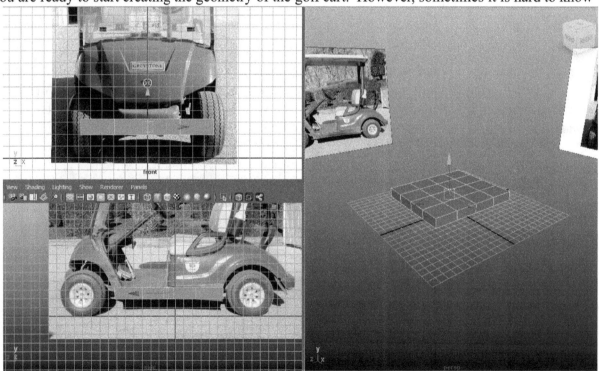

*Figure: 2.08*

where to start modeling. The best method is to try to identify basic geometric shapes that make up the object you want to model. Parts of the golf cart can actually be constructed by simply moving, scaling, and rotating the primitive shapes provided in Maya. The steering column and steering wheel are not much more than an elongated polygon cylinder and a torus with a few cubes to connect it all together.

When you have these simple solutions available to you, take advantage of them. But most of the model is made up of more complicated geometry. Start with the large, general shapes and refine the detail afterward.

*Figure: 2.09*

Let's start the base of the golf cart by creating a polygon primitive cube and transforming it with the move, rotate, and scale tools until it lines up with the floor of the golf cart from the front wheel well to the rear wheel well.

Now in the channel box under *INPUTS*, select *polyCube1*, and change *Subdivision Width* to 4, *Subdivision Height* to 1, and *Subdivision Depth* to 4, as shown in Figure: 2.08.

Alter the model to align with the base a little more accurately by right clicking on the box and choosing the *Vertex* sub-object. In the side view, marquee select an entire line of vertices by left mouse dragging to create a marquee selection box. Use the move tool to line them up with the black area that makes up the floor of the cart and the black trim below the seat. When you are done, you should have something resembling Figure: 2.09.

Next, you are going to continue blocking out the basic shapes of the golf cart. Start by creating the area

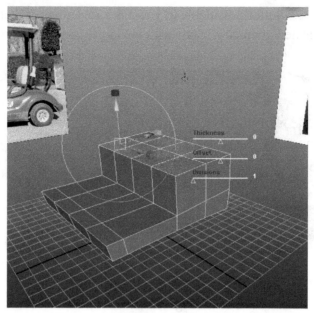

*Figure: 2.10*

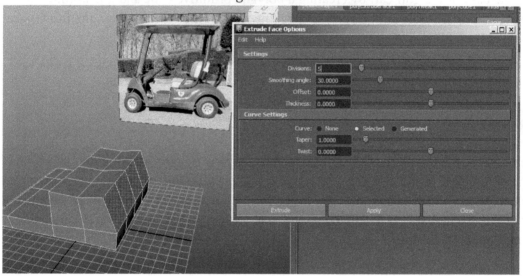

*Figure: 2.11*

under the seat, above the floor you just created. But rather than create that out of a new object you will use a new tool called *Extrude*.

In the sub-object level, choose *face*, and in the perspective view, select the eight faces that are directly below the seat of the golf cart. In the *Polygon* menu set, click *Edit Mesh>Extrude*. You will notice that your manipulator now looks different. This new manipulator allows you to move, rotate, and scale the extrusion all with one tool. Be careful to not press the "Q," "W," "E," or "R" keys during this time. Doing so will cause you to lose access to the extrude manipulator.

Select the Z translate handle (the blue one), and move it upward until it lines up with the bottom or the seats in the side view. The result should resemble Figure: 2.10. Again, in the side view, align the vertices to the shape under the seat.

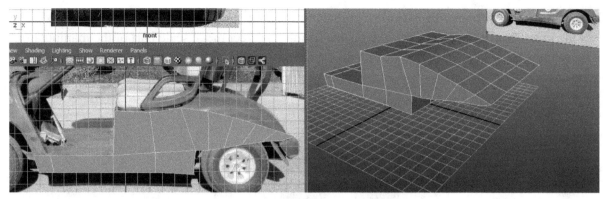

Figure: 2.12

Now select the four faces along the back (on the area you just extruded), and choose the tool settings options (the little square) at the end of the *Edit Mesh>Extrude* menu item. Change *Divisions* to 5, and click *Extrude*.

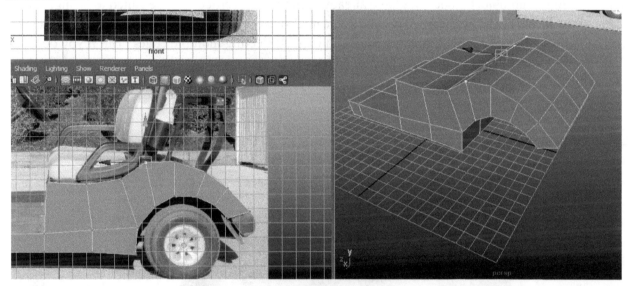

Figure: 2.13

Use the extrude manipulator to move the face in the Z axis. You will see that the section you have extruded has 5 divisions in it. The next time you use the extrude tool the settings will default to the last

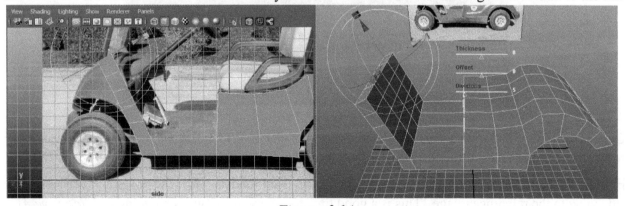

Figure: 2.14

used settings, so your next extrude will also have 5 divisions unless you specify differently.

Select the blue circle around the extrude manipulator to rotate the extruded face in the red X axis. Select the green box at the end of the Y translate handle to select the Y scale part of the manipulator. Use these three tools to position the extruded face along the golf cart's bumper in the side view.

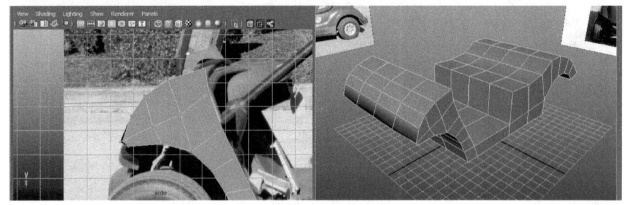

*Figure: 2.15*

Select the *Edge* sub-object mode. We have already seen that the vertices can be edited to change the shape of the mesh, but as you learned earlier, you can also manipulate the edges to shape the model. You can select a line of edges by holding Shift and toggle-selecting multiple edges. But if you double-click an edge, you will select an entire loop of edges.

Use the different sub-object modes to manipulate the mesh to line up with the rear fender of the golf cart, as shown in Figure: 2.13.

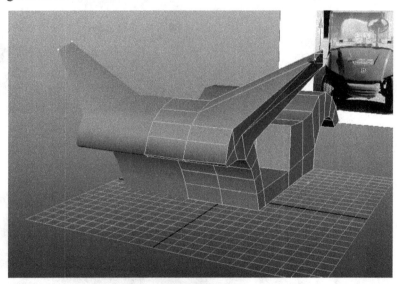

*Figure: 2.16*

Create the front of the golf cart using the same methods you used to create the rear fender. Extrude the forward-most four faces of the floor upward to create the dashboard.

Extrude the eight top-most faces to create the hood and front fender. Align the edges and vertices in the side view to the reference image. This is a good time to save your progress by going to *File>Save As*. Save the file as "Golf_Cart_01.mb". **It is important to remember to save multiple iterations of**

**your file as you work instead of resaving over the same file in case a file becomes corrupt.**

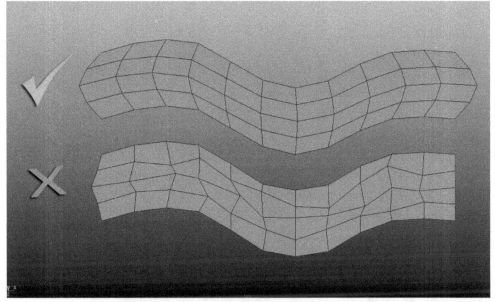

*Figure: 2.17*

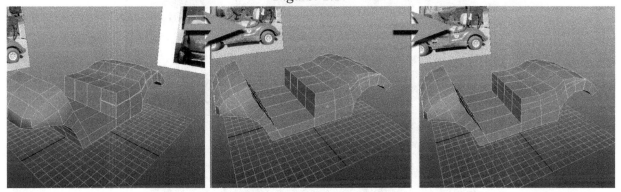

*Figure: 2.18*

You now have a blocked-out model of the golf cart's base. The next step will be to refine the shape and add in additional details. Up to this point, the majority of the shaping of the model has happened in the side orthographic view. The result is a boxy, rigid form when viewed in perspective.

To soften this shape, we will, once again, return to the sub-object menu to manipulate and form the model. This is a good time to bring up the old adage "Work smarter, not harder." You will notice that the golf cart's base is symmetrical across the X axis. So rather than model both sides and try to make them identical we will let Maya do it for us.

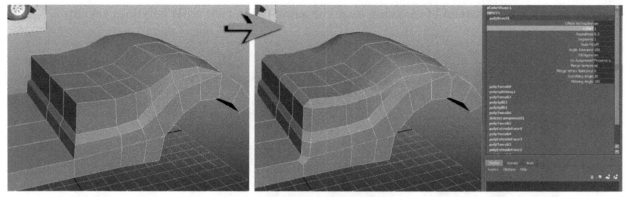

*Figure: 2.20*

In the front view, go to *Face* sub-object mode and marquee select the left half of the model's faces, and

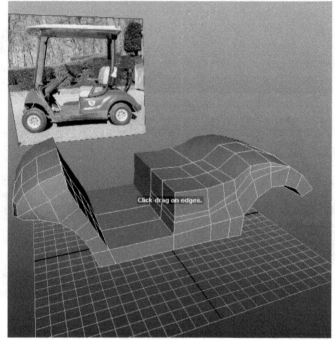

*Figure: 2.19*

press the delete key. In the perspective view, you will now see that you only have half of a model. Now if you make changes to this half, you can simply create a mirror image of the mesh to have a symmetrical model. But mirroring is usually done closer to the end of the modeling process, and it is difficult to visualize the entire form when all you can see is one half of it.

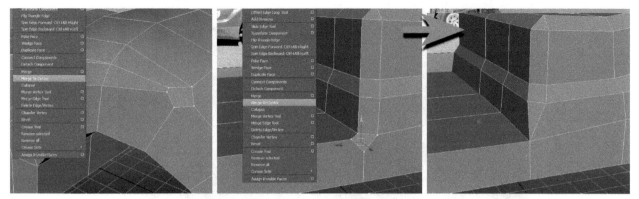

*Figure: 2.21*

To rectify this problem, we are going to create a mirrored instance of the right half of the model. An instance is a special kind of copy that receives the same updates to the form as the original. Select the remaining half of the golf cart base, and go to *Edit>Duplicate Special*, and select the options box (the square box to the right). Under *Geometry type,* choose *Instance* and under *Scale X*, type -1. Click *Duplicate Special*. You will now see that the original mesh has been duplicated across the X axis (or scaled to negative 1) and that if you select a sub-object on the original mesh, you can make edits that will automatically update on the new, duplicated mesh.

You can now start the process of refining the form of the golf cart base. First, move individual vertices and edges in the X axis to soften the sharp edge on the front fender. One of the cornerstones to the modeling process is manually shaping vertices, edges, and faces to refine a model's form. This is where you have to use your powers of observation. Refer to the reference and be sure to tumble around

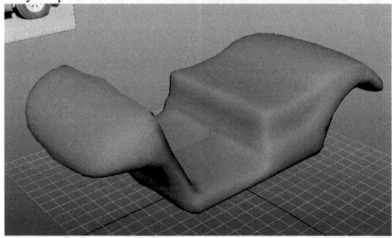

*Figure: 2.22*

the model often to make sure the edits you are making to the geometry look good from all angles. Also, try to keep the flow of edges sensible and even across the model as shown in Figure: 2.17.

Repeat the refining of the form on the rear end of the golf cart as well. Keep in mind that this is just a blocking out of the overall form. **Save your progress.**

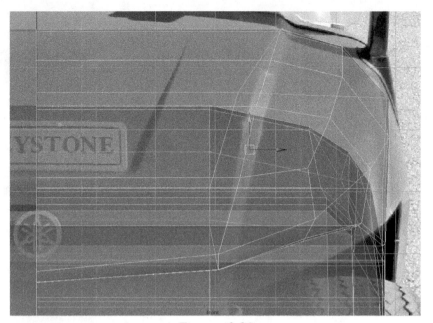

*Figure: 2.25*

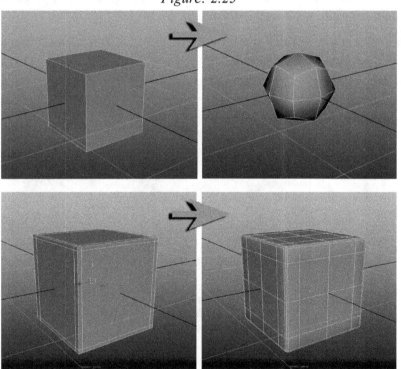

*Figure: 2.23*

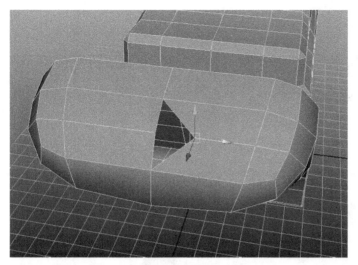

*Figure: 2.26*

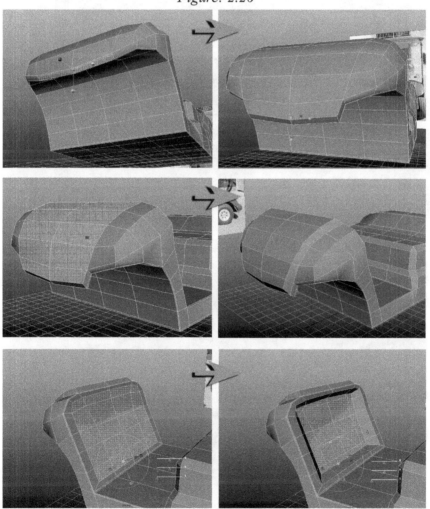

*Figure: 2.27*

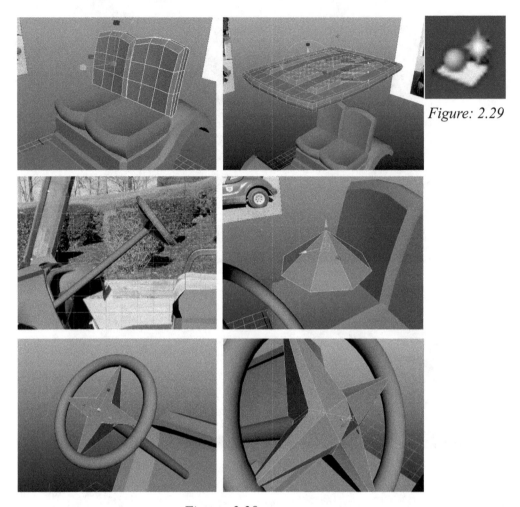

Figure: 2.29

Figure: 2.28

Now that we have altered the form to be more natural, the next step is to start adding refinement. We

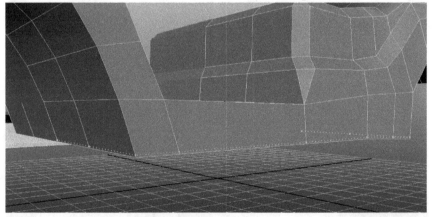

Figure: 2.24

will do this by adding additional edges where we need them. Go to *Edit Mesh>Interactive Split Tool*. This tool will allow you to manually draw additional edges on the mesh. Start creating this new edge by clicking in the top corner of the top edge, above the rear wheel well. Create the edge around the front of the area below the seat by clicking from edge to edge. Do not worry about the placement yet, we will alter that later. When you get to the center of the mesh, press the enter key to create the edge.

Now create a second edge right above the new edge you just created. When you are done, you should have two very similar edges, side by side, as shown in Figure: 2.18.

Now, in the side view, adjust the edges to line up with the contour on the reference image by adjusting the vertices and edges. One helpful tip is to select *Shading>XRay* from the panels menu. This will turn your model translucent, allowing you to still see the model's form and the reference image behind it at the same time.

You will find that you do not have quite enough vertices to define the contour clearly. To correct, go to *Edit Mesh>Insert Edge Loop Tool*, and click on the top edge of the second face back, below the seat. As you can see, this tool inserts an edge that travels along the flow of the face you selected. The interactive split tool and the insert edge loop tool are both very powerful ways of adding additional edges for refining your model's shape. After the edge loop is in place, adjust the new vertices to align with the contour on the reference image.

Now, move the topmost faces in, slightly, to create the indented upper area. **Save your work.**

The area under the seat is feeling very rigid, so to add a little bit more detail, we are going to use a new tool. Select the corner edges of the boxy region under the seat all the way back to the insertion point on the two new edges you just created. Go to *Edit Mesh>Bevel*. You will see that the single edge doubled into two edges. In the channel box under *INPUTS*, expand the *polyBevel1* node, and enter 1 into the *Offset* channel. This will widen the two edges further apart, rounding off the sharp edge. Notice it is possible to add additional segments to the bevel in the input node, but one should be enough here.

Now you will want to do a little bit of cleanup on the mesh. The bevel tool often leaves unwanted

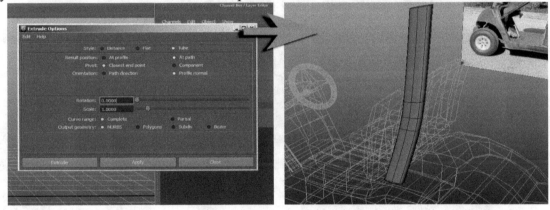

*Figure: 2.31*

edges that will cause you problems when you smooth. All your faces need to be either three or four

Figure: 2.32

sided.  In some areas, we can merge vertices together by selecting them and using the interactive split tool to turn five sided faces into a four and a three sided face.  Check the mesh thoroughly to eliminate any faces that exceed four edges by using *Edit Mesh>Merge to Center*.


At this time, it may be hard to imagine how this boxy, faceted model will ever look like the smooth glossy cart in the reference images.  It is important to remember that eventually the model will be smoothed.  **Save** a copy of your file now, and let's explore the effects of smoothing on your model.

With the model selected, go to *Mesh>Smooth*.  You will see the sharp edges on your model were rounded off and the amount of edges on the mesh doubled.  This smooth addresses our issue earlier of feeling too boxy but now the entire model feels like a fluffy balloon, which is an equally unsatisfactory result.

But the results from the smooth tool are actually very predictable once you understand how it works. In the illustration below, you will see two cubes and the resulting new mesh after having a smooth applied to them.  If two edges are close together, they will smooth with a much more crisp edge.  Whereas the cube with large spaces between the edges has its edges rounded so much that it almost creates a sphere.

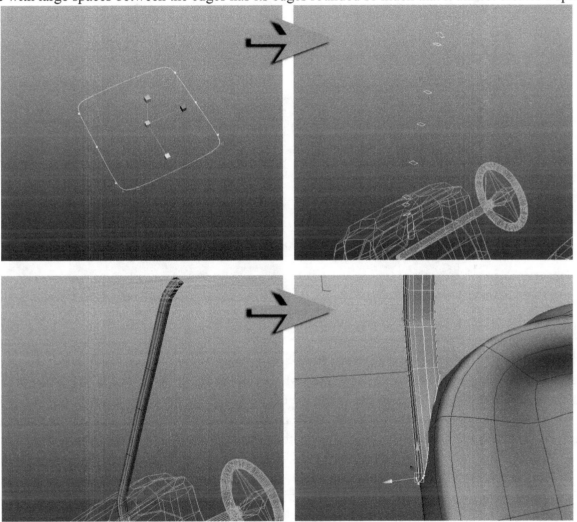

*Figure: 2.33*

Adjusting the length between two edges changes the amount the smooth tool will round off the edges. If you want an edge to stay sharp after the smooth, place another edge very close to it.

Let's get back to our golf cart.  Press Ctrl + Z to undo the smooth.   If you would like to see a preview version of what the model would look like smoothed, you can press the 3 key.  This is not the actual smooth; instead this is a preview of what the model would look like as a subdivision surface.

A subdivision surface is another type of geometry that Maya allows you to create. It is a sort of hybrid between a polygon and NURBS object.  Although subdivision surfaces are very powerful modeling tools, many of the basics of polygon modeling apply to them as well. So we will not be exploring them in this book.

So let's take a little time to sharpen up the edges that we want to remain rigid. Press 1 to go back into the non-subdivided view. Sharpen up the bottom edge of the golf cart base using the insert edge loop

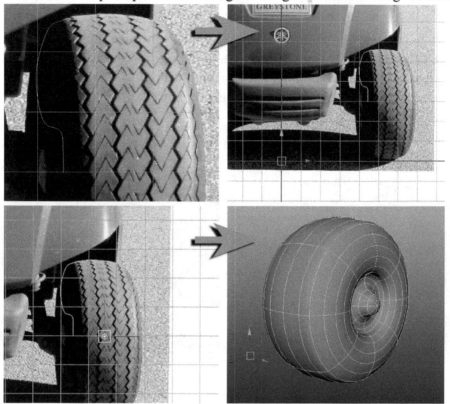

*Figure: 2.34*

tool. Insert the new edge very close, but not on top, of the bottom most edge. If you view the subdivided mode, you will see the bottom most edge is much sharper now.

We also want to sharpen up the inside edge of the wheel well by using a new tool. Double click the edge along the inside of the wheel well to select the edge loop. Most likely the entire wheel well edge will not be selected, but this will select many of the edges. Hold shift to toggle select the remaining edges. While holding shift down again, also select the inner edge of the rear wheel well and the bottom

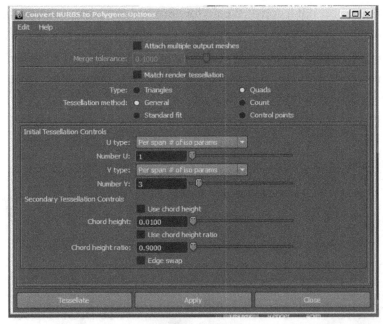

*Figure: 2.35*

*Figure: 2.36*

of the rear end where the base connects to the rear bumper. Also, select the corner floor edges and the inside dashboard edge. These are all the edges we want to remain sharp after the smooth. Go to *Edit Mesh>Bevel*, and set the *Offset* to 0.1. If you press 3, you will see the edges are now sharper. **Save an iteration of the file.**

In the front view, adjust the second edge on the hood to line up with the raised area in the reference image. You can use the *Shading>Xray* option to help you see the underlying reference image.

The last few additions we need to make pertain to the center of the model. To prevent destroying the clean seam along the center of the mesh, let's re-merge the two sides of the model. Recall that the left side of the mesh is an instance, not a copy. We no longer want the instanced version of the model, so delete it in order to create asymmetry.

Now go to *Edit Mesh>Mirror Geometry*, and select the options box. Check *-X* in the mirror direction, and uncheck *Merge with the Original*. We uncheck this option because often close vertices are wrongfully merged with this option check. Click *Mirror*.

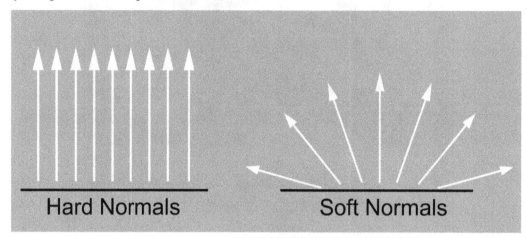

*Figure: 2.37*

You will see that although the model is one mesh the center vertices are not connected, as illustrated in Figure: 2.26. In the front view, marquee select all the center vertices then go to *Edit Mesh>Merge*.

After the mirror is complete, use the extrude tool to make the raised hood area and to indent the dash panel as shown in the below illustrations.

Create the seats and roof using the same techniques used in modeling the base. Create the cushions by making a cube and altering the form by editing the sub-objects. Create the roof using the extrude tool

*Figure: 2.38*

and the insert edge loop tool. The steering column, steering wheel, and pedals are simply polygon primitives that you can slightly alter as needed. **Save your work.**

The scene is now getting pretty crowded. Let's organize the mesh into a layer. At the bottom of the channel box is the layer editor. Select all of the objects in the scene. Now click the icon pictured in Figure: 2.29 to create a new layer containing the selected objects. You will see the *Layer1* appear below. Double-click on *Layer1* to open the edit layer options. Name the layer "Polygons," and click save.

Back in the layer editor, you will see three boxes. The first box has a *V* in it. Clicking this box will turn the visibility of the layer on and off. The second box is empty. If you click it once, a *T* will appear. The *T* stands for "Templated," meaning the objects in the layer are not selectable and you can only see a gray wireframe of the mesh in the workspace. If you click this column again, the *T* will become an *R* which stands for "Referenced." Referenced layers are completely visible in the workspace, but you cannot select or edit them. Turn this layer to templated mode.

## *NURBS modeling*

Now that we have explored the power of polygon modeling, let's explore the creative capabilities of NURBS.

Go to *Create>CV Curve*, and in the side view, create a curve that lines up with the center of the rear roof support pillar.

Under *Create>NURBS Primitives*, uncheck *Interactive Creation*, then create a NURBS circle by going to *Create>NURBS Primitives>Circle*. In the side view, move the newly created circle to the base of the CV curve.

Select the circle, and in the perspective view, select *Show>Isolate Select>View Selected* from the panel menu. You will see that only the circle is now visible. This is a nice way to eliminate the surrounding clutter, temporarily, while you focus on the details of the model.

Scale and move the control vertices of the circle to shape it into a rounded rectangle as shown in Figure: 2.30. Exit out of the isolate selected mode by un-checking Show>*Isolate Select>View Selected.*

Select the two curves and move them in the X axis to the driver's side of the cart. Use the front reference view as well as the perspective view to align the curves in an appropriate location.

Select the circle then the CV curve. It is important to select them in this order. Under the *Surfaces* menu set, go to *Surfaces>Extrude*, and select the options box. In the options, check *At Path* in the *Result Position* option and *Profile Normal* in the *Orientation* option. Click *Extrude*.

Sometimes the loft is not perfect. At this time, you can alter the extrusion's sub-objects to align the form to the reference image more accurately.

To refine the pillar, we are going to add more isoparms. Isoparms are the curves on the surface of the NURBS object that create the form. Right click on the mesh, and select the *Isoparm* sub-object type. Select the top most isoparm, and drag it along the surface of the NURBS object. You will see a dotted line indicating the placement of the new isoparm. Hold shift and repeat this process again, creating a second isoparm near the one you just created. To finish the process go to *Edit NURBS>Insert Isoparms*. Now you can edit the control vertices to refine the form of the pillar.

Next select the NURBS pillar, and go to *Edit>Delete by Type> History*. This breaks the history connection between the curves and the final NURBS extrusion. You can now delete the two creation curves. To mirror the pillar, duplicate it with the shortcut Ctrl + D. In the channel box, change the *Scale X* from 1 to -1.

To create the front roof pillar, create another NURBS circle. In the channel box *INPUT* node, change the number of *Sections* from 8 to 16. This will give you more control vertices to alter on the circle. Shape the circle into a rounded square. In the side view, duplicate the square aligning them incrementally along the shape of the front pillar. Rotate and scale the bottom most square to the shape of pillar base.

Select all of the squares. Again, the order of selection is important. Select them one at a time from the bottom up. Go to *Surfaces>Loft*.

Edit any control vertices needed to refine the form. Move the pillar to the driver's side of the cart base. Alter the bottom of the NURBS surface to fit the contour of the cart base. Delete the objects history, and delete the construction curves. Duplicate the mesh. Because you lofted this object in the center, simply scaling the object to -1 in the X axis only mirrors it on the driver's side of the cart. You must also change the *Translate X* to a negative of its current value.

To create the wheel of the golf cart, we are going to go to the front view and dolly in on the driver side tire. With the CV curve tool, draw a profile view of the tire and wheel. Refer to the other reference images to determine the shape of the areas you cannot see in the front view.

To create the tire, you will want to revolve this curve, but the revolve tool rotates the curve around the object's pivot point. You will notice that the curves manipulator is at the origin, not at the center of the tire. Press the insert key on your keyboard. Now you will be able to alter the object's pivot point location and rotation. Move it to the center of the tire. Press "Q," "W," "E," or "R" to exit the pivot point editing mode.

Now select the curve, and go to *Surface>Revolve* to create the NURBS surface of the tire and wheel. Duplicate and place the other three tires. **Save the file**.

To make texturing easier, you can convert the NURBS surfaces to polygons by selecting the NURBS object and going to *Modify>Convert>NURBS to Polygons* and selecting the options box. For the NURBS objects you created in this project the setting shown in Figure: 2.35 works very well for the conversion.

Now we are going to explore creating a quick environment for your golf cart. Create a polygon plane, and under the *polyPlane1* node, change the *Width* and *Height* to 300 and the *Subdivision Width* and *Subdivision Height* to 50. With the plane selected, go to *Mesh> Sculpt Geometry Tool*, and choose the options box. The tools settings will open.

You will see that as you mouse over the plane your cursor now appears as a brush and a small red circle on the surface of the plane. Click-dragging along the mesh will cause the mesh to deform. This tool can be used to quickly alter a mesh as if you were sculpting.

In the tools settings window, you will see that you can change the size of the brush by raising the *Radius(U)* value. Also note that this value can be changed in the workspace by holding down "B" and left-click-dragging.

Under the *Sculpt Parameters*, you can change the *Operations* from Push, Pull, Smooth, Relax, Pinch, and Erase. The *Max. displacement* value allows you to adjust the strength of the selected operation. The best way to learn how this tool works is to experiment with it, so take this time to sculpt a ground plane suitable for your golf cart.

Add details to the cart and environment at your own discretion. Some additional details to consider adding are bumpers, axles, and arm rests. Make the model your own. This is your chance to explore the modeling tools and what you can do with them.

Before you call the model complete, make sure you have named each model appropriately. This seems like a trivial task, but correct naming is crucial in a production environment. Scenes become complex very quickly and having the objects in the scene named clearly will allow you to organize and understand your scene better. It will make your life much easier later on in the production pipeline. If you have to pass the scene off to another artist, it is important for them to be able to interpret what is happening in the file quickly. Nothing is more frustrating than opening a coworker's scene and finding 200 objects all named pCube.

## Normals

One quick last topic to cover in this chapter is normals. As mentioned earlier, all polygon edges are straight lines, meaning that all faces are flat. In nature flat surfaces reflect light based on their shape. But in Maya, the decision on how the light will interact with the faces of your model is controlled by the normals. A hard normal means that light will bounce off the face as if it is flat. Softened normals react as if they are rounded on the edges.

Normals can be used to imply sharp edges are softer than they are, allowing lower resolution models to appear less blocky. To see how this works in practice, create a polygon cube in a new Maya scene. The cube's normals are hard by default. Select the model, and in the *Polygon* menu set, go to *Normals>Soften Edges*.

As you can see, the lighting bounces off the faces in a way that makes the box feel rounded. Now go to *Normals>Harden Edges*. Hardening normals is a good way to emphasize sharper corners on your mesh.

A process known as normal mapping is often used to manipulate the normals to imply detail that is not present in the actual mesh. Third party programs such as Autodesk's Mudbox or Pixologic's Zbrush are used to create extremely high resolution versions of the model. Then a normal map of the high resolution detail is applied to a lower resolution version of the model. This allows the modeler to insert fine details without driving up the polygon count.

Modeling is challenging, but it can also be tremendously rewarding. An immense feeling of accomplishment comes with the knowledge that you started with nothing, an empty Maya scene, and now you have a finished model. It is that feeling of accomplishment that turns hobbyists into enthusiasts and enthusiasts into career professionals. Be careful, it is addictive.

# Chapter 3: Texturing

Congratulations! You have completed your first model. Step back, and breathe in the pride that comes with creation. You started with a simple six-sided box, and now you have an intricately-crafted golf cart.

But it won't take long for you to realize that despite all of your hard work on this model, it's gray. Your model is a dull color, but you can change it. By understanding why your model is gray and how to enhance it, you can add the splash of paint and the spark of realism to your work. Let's start with the basics.

## *Materials*

**Save** the most current iteration of your model, and then create a new scene by going to *File>New Scene*. In this new scene, create a polygon cube, a polygon sphere, a polygon cylinder, and a polygon plane, and move them side by side so they are not all on top of each other.

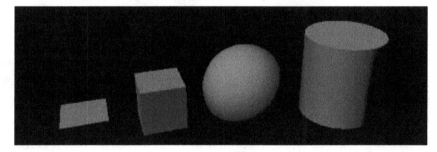

*Figure: 3.01*

Select the sphere, and in the attribute editor, click the arrow buttons at the far right of the node tabs until you get to a node called *lambert1*. Select the *lambert1* tab to expand it in the attribute editor. This is the material that is on your cube, sphere, cylinder, and plane.

Yes, you read that correctly. This same material is on all four of the objects in your scene. Under the *Common Material Attributes* dropdown click on the gray box beside *Color*, and use the color picker to choose a bright red. Notice that all three objects in the workspace turned red.

In Maya, a material is a separate node that you can connect to geometry. This allows you to change one material and update it across every object in your scene with the same material. If an object's material were simply an attribute of that individual mesh, changing an army of 5000 pink robots to an army of 5000 blue robots would be a task that would take hours or even days. With the material being a separate node, as it is in Maya, that task only takes a few seconds.

When you create a new scene in Maya, the scene comes with a lambert1 material already created. When you create a new object, Maya connects the lambert1 material to the new object, so it will be viewable. By default, all geometry, including your golf cart, has the lambert1 material on it.

But what is a material? The edges and vertices that make up the model are just mathematical data. For an object to be visible, it has to have a material to tell Maya the proper way to display the surface of the object. Is the object glossy and reflective or is it dull and gritty? Is the object a solid color throughout or is it covered in detailed designs? The material provides that information to Maya, so the object can be rendered correctly.

The default Maya material, lambert1, is a Lambert material. A Lambert material is only one of several kinds of materials that you can create in Maya. Lambert, Blinn, Phong, Phong E, and Anisotropic are some of the other types of basic materials Maya offers to help you create the surface of your model. Each is a different type of shading algorithm that provides you with different material options. Lambert is the simplest one. It provides you with only a diffuse color, no specularity or reflections. This material type is usually on models that have a matte finish.

Let's explore some of the other material types in the *Hypershade*. The hypershade is the editor in which you can create, modify, and attach new materials. To open the hypershade, you will go to *Window>Render Editors>Hypershade*. The daunting complexity of the hypershade is misleading. Let's focus on the hypershade top where you will see three materials. The first material is the default lambert1 material. The other two are effects materials. The hypershade top is where you can find all of the materials and hypershade-editable nodes in your scene. The area directly below the hypershade top is the work area. This is where we can do detailed node work to our materials. We will come back to this area. The vertical list to the left is the create bar. This is the list of nodes that can be created in the hypershade.

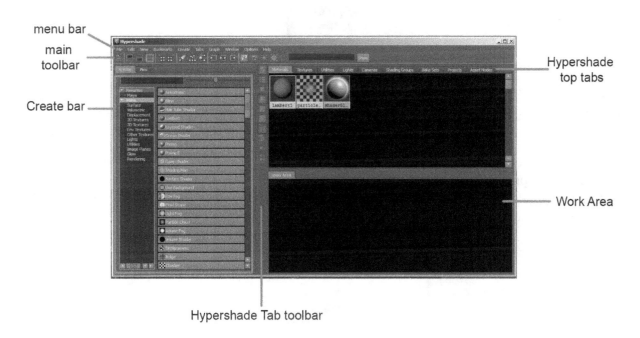

*Figure: 3.02*

You will notice at the top of the create bar node list is the Anisotropic and Blinn materials as previously mentioned. Click on each of them to create one of each of the new materials. A new Anisotropic and Blinn material should appear in both the hypershade top and the work area.

Resize the hypershade window, so you can see the two new materials and your workspace camera view of the four polygon objects at the same time. Marquee select the four polygon objects. In the work area of the hypershade, hold down right-click on the newly created Blinn material. A marking menu will pop up around your mouse. Drag up to select *Assign Material to Selection*. Now the Blinn material has been assigned to all four pieces of geometry.

In the workspace, the new material may not look much different from the default lambert1 material. But you will notice that the objects have a glossier shine to them. The workspace is not the best way to view materials though.

In the status line, you will see a row of icons that resemble movie clapboards. These are the render buttons. We will explore them more in the lighting and rendering chapter, but for now click the second button from the left, the one that looks like a plain blank clapper. The render view window will pop up and do a quick software render of the active camera view.

*Figure: 3.03*

In the render, you will be able to clearly see the specular highlight on the ball. The Blinn material works well at showing highlights on rounded surfaces. Press the green button to the right of the 1:1 icon in the render view toolbar. This will temporarily save the image in the render view so you can compare it to others.

*Figure:*
*3.04*

Try adding the Anisotropic material to the objects and rendering again. You will see that the specular highlight on the ball and cylinder are elongated. Anisotropic is good for objects that need a long contour-shaped highlight. Click the green keep image button again, and now you can drag the scroll bar at the bottom of the render view to flip between the two images and compare them.

For reference purposes, create a new Lambert shader in the hypershade and apply it to the objects. Render and click the keep image button. Flip through the three images (also shown in Figure: 3.05). Note that the flat surfaces, for the most part, do not change much.

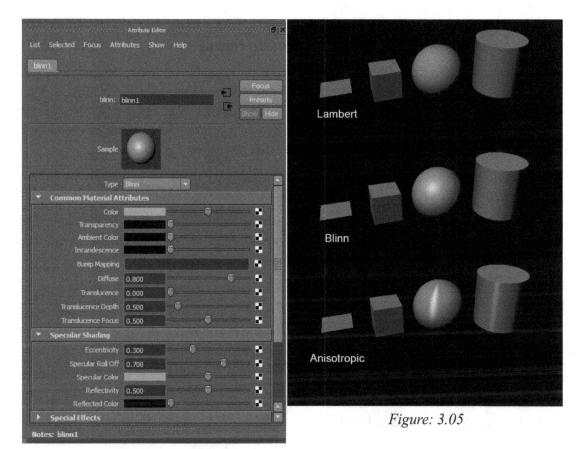

Figure: 3.05

Figure: 3.06

Reapply the Blinn material to the four objects, and let's explore some of the things you can do with the material attributes. In the attribute editor, you should see something similar to Figure: 3.06.

For good practices, let's rename this material from blinn1 to "MyMaterial" by clicking in the input box at the top. It is always strongly advised that you name your materials so you do not get confused later.

Notice that you can drag the slider in the *Transparency* option and the objects or more accurately the material becomes translucent.

*Ambient Color* blends with the *Diffuse* color. The lighter the ambient color the brighter the overall color of the object. This is a difficult blend to perfect so for now leave ambient color set to the default.

*Incandescence* is essentially self-illumination. The brighter the incandescence the more the object appears to create its own light.

Let's jump further down to the *Specular Shading* section. *Eccentricity* controls the size of the highlight while *Specular Roll Off* gives the material different reflective abilities. *Specular Color* changes the color of the specular highlight.

Although we have reflectivity options on this material, you will not be able to see reflections in the render right now. For reflections to show up, some of the rendering options have to be changed. We will explore rendering options in the lighting and rendering chapter.

Let's go back up to the *Color* option. Earlier we saw that we could change the material's color but that is not the only way we are limited to adjusting the colors that appear on the material. At the end of the slider in the color attribute is a small checkered square. Click on that square. The *Create Render Node Window* will pop up. Choose the *Checker* node by clicking on it once.

Now it may appear as if nothing happened. Earlier in the first chapter we learned that you can change the shading option of the camera view to wireframe by pressing 4 and that you can view the object in shaded view by pressing 5. If you press 6 on the keyboard, you can now view the geometry in textured mode. As you can see, the checker texture was applied to the objects. Press the quick render button to see a higher quality render of the textured model.

You will see that your attribute editor has also changed. Now you are viewing the *checker1* node and that is accompanied by a *place2dTexture1* node.

Let's go back to the hypershade to explore what is happening with this material. In the hypershade top, right click and hold on *MyMaterial* until the marking menu comes up and then choose *Graph Network*. This will expand out the selected material's node network in the work area.

As you can see, we have three nodes that make up this material. *MyMaterial* is the Blinn material we created and renamed. You will see another node to the left of it called *checker1*. Notice that a small green arrow is connecting *checker1* to *MyMaterial*.

If you mouse over the green arrow, you will see the follow text:

*checker1.outColor -> MyMaterial.color.*

Basically this means that the output color of the checker1 node is filling the color attribute of MyMaterial. If you select this checker1 node, you can change the color of the checker pattern in the attribute editor.

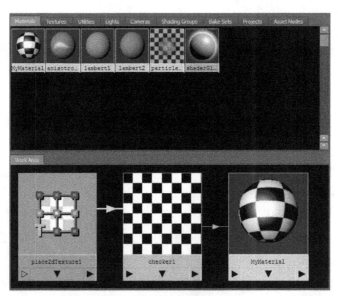

Figure: 3.07

The *place2dTexure1* node is telling the *checker1* node how it should be placed on the object. If you select the place2dTexture1 node and look at it in the attribute editor, you will see that you can change many of the placement options. For example, if you change the values in *Repeat UV* to 8 and 8, the checker pattern becomes a lot smaller on the objects in the scene.

Select *MyMaterial*, and view it in the attribute editor. Let's remove the checker texture from the material by right-clicking on the word *Color* and choosing *Break Connection*.

Five attributes down the list you will see the words *Bump Mapping*. A bump map is a texture that renders small raised and lowered details. The mesh is not actually changed but the object is rendered in a way to make it appear as if it has fine details.

Click on the checkerboard square to bring up the create render node window and choose *Fractal*. Bump maps are not viewable in the camera view so to see the results of this bump map click on the quick render button. You should have something similar to the image in Figure: 3.08.

*Figure: 3.08*

In MyMaterial, remove the bump map by right-clicking on the word *Bump Mapping* and choosing *Break Connection*.

One last thing to explore in MyMaterial's attributes. Select the checkerboard square to open the create render node window. This time choose *File*. In the attribute editor under *Image Name*, click the folder at the end of the input box. Navigate your computer and point it toward any digital photo or image you may have stored on your computer.

Click the quick render button to see a software render of the objects. The material now has the image you selected as its color. You can create images or use images you photograph yourself to texture your 3D models. Also note that you can map images to other material attributes as well. You can create your own specular and bump maps too.

*Figure: 3.09*

## UV's

The ability to create your own texture maps opens you up to a world of creative options. But as you may have noticed from the previous section, the image you choose may not be placed perfectly, or even logically, on the surface of the model. The problem you face in the process of texturing is that your model exists in three dimensions while the image is two dimensional.

To illustrate the complications that this creates, think of wrapping a present with wrapping paper. Wrapping boxy shapes like a dvd or cd case is simple. Flat surfaces and right angles are easy shapes in which to contort a flat piece of paper. But imagine trying to gift wrap a tricycle. Even something as simple as a basketball is difficult to wrap neatly because of the rounded shape. Imagine the difficulty of trying to wrap a living creature, such as a frog, a puppy, or a human being (please do not actually attempt this).

To align a 2D image on the surface of a 3D object, Maya and many other 3D packages use a process called UV mapping. UV mapping allows you to specify where parts of a 2D image will be placed on the 3D model by allowing you to realign the wireframe of your model in a theoretical 2D space. This 2D space is used as a road map for how the image should wrap around the model. The letters U and V are used as coordinate axes because X, Y, and Z were already taken.

Go to *Window>UV Texture Editor*. The window that opens is the theoretical 2D workspace where you can adjust the way the 2D image will align to the 3D model. Select the plane, the cube, the sphere, and the cylinder in turn to see how the mesh's UV's are unwrapped. Many of the UV layouts make sense, and almost resemble the geometry they represent while others seem confusing and tangled.

A way to think of UV layout is to imagine your model is made of paper, and you wish to print an image on it. But it will not go through the printer unless it is flat, so your job is to strategically slice the model up in such a way as to allow it to be flattened and sent through the printer.

The cube looks as if it has simply been sliced down the corners and unfolded flat. The cylinder's UV

*Figure: 3.11*

layout looks as if the caps were neatly detached and then it was sliced down one side so it could be

*Figure: 3.10*

rolled out flat. The plane is flat already so its UV placement is simple.

The sphere is a less direct interpretation. This is because the sphere is curved. Back to our paper and printer analogy, cutting a sphere is difficult unless you are able to stretch the paper to flatten it out. Effectively that is what you have to do when laying out the UV's for rounded, curved objects. It is a delicate balance. Too much or too little stretching and the texture map will become distorted. Keeping a smooth and even edge flow in the UV layout helps minimize distortion.

Select the cube, and in the UV texture editor, right click on the wireframe and choose UV. This is the only sub-object that can be edited in the UV texture editor because it is the only one that exists in UV space. Vice versa, the UV sub-object cannot be edited in 3D space. Think of each UV as a reference on the 2D image for each of the model's vertices.

You can marquee select corners of the wireframe to select UV's. As in the workspace, the short-cut keys "W," "E," and "R" allow you to manipulate the UV's. You can also use the same Alt + mouse button navigational controls to track and dolly in the editor. The menu and toolbar at the top of the UV texture editor contains many valuable tools you can use to layout your model's UV's.

Let's start laying out the UV's on your golf cart model. Open the most recent save file. Set the menu set menu to *Polygons*.

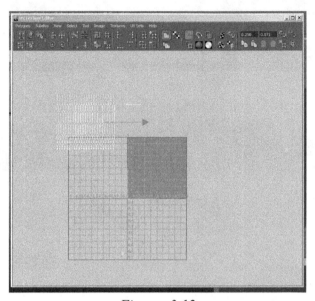

Figure: 3.12

Before starting the unwrapping process, make sure that no smoothing is on the object. If you smoothed the object before saving, you can find the *polySmoothFace* node in either the channel box INPUT section or the attribute editor. Set *Divisions* to 0.

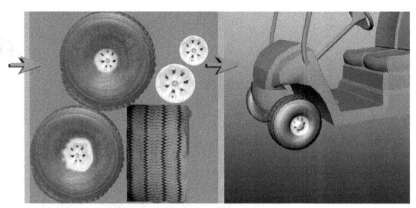

*Figure: 3.16*

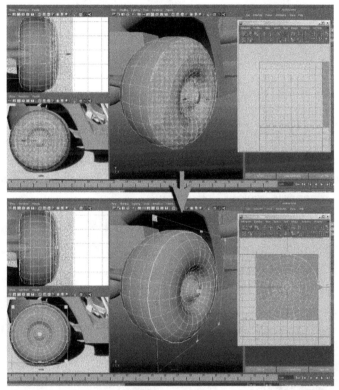

*Figure: 3.13*

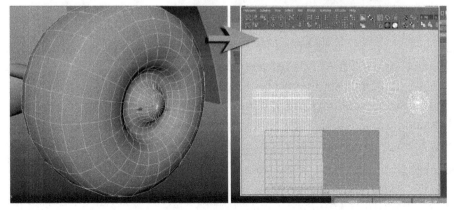

*Figure: 3.14*

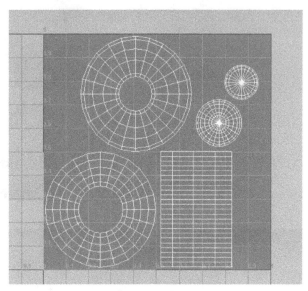

*Figure: 3.15*

You can also hide the image planes by selecting the front and side cameras in the outliner and pressing Ctrl+H.

In the workspace, marquee select all the mesh in your scene, and go to *Edit>Delete by Type>History*. This removes all the creation nodes and gives you a clean model history. Modeling history can sometimes cause problems with the UV's. Also go to *Modify>Freeze Transformations*. This resets the translate, rotate, and scale channels back to their default.

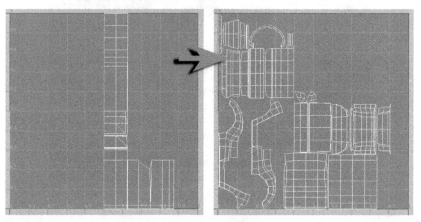

*Figure: 3.17*

First, let's layout the UV's of the wheel (the tire and rim). Select the wheel model and open the UV texture editor. When laying out the UV's on a model, the goal is to arrange them in a way which will be easiest to create a texture map for the mesh. As you can see, right now the UV layout is not very easy to understand. To successfully create a texture map for the wheel, you need to be able to tell where the tread should be, where the walls of the tires are, and where the center caps are. So the goal of laying out these UV's is to make it easy to decipher.

To get a good starting point, let's use one of Maya's create UV mapping tools. These tools are found under the create UV's menu item. The first five menu options are your choices: *Planar Mapping, Cylindrical Mapping, Spherical Mapping, Automatic Mapping, and Create UV's Based on Camera*. These options allow you to project the mapping coordinates based on predefined shapes. If you were to choose planar mapping from a side view of the tire, your UV's would resemble the wireframe view of the wheel from an orthographic side view.

The wheel most closely resembles a cylinder, so let's use the cylindrical mapping option to get us to a starting point. A cylindrical UV manipulator will appear around the wheel, but we need to alter it to make it wrap around the wheel in the correct direction. In the channel box, on the *PolyCylProj1* node, set the *Rotate Z* to 90, the *Projection Horizontal Sweep* to 320, and the *Projection Height* to 3.

As you can see in the UV texture editor, the layout is still confusing. The cylindrical mapping only gets you to a good starting point. Although it is hard to see, the tread portion of the tire is pretty much

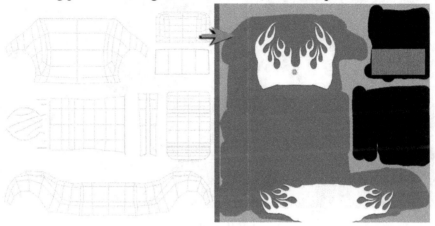

*Figure: 3.18*

complete, but the front and back of the tire was also projected from the cylindrical angle as well, making it unreadable to the camera.

In the UV Texture editor, right-click and select *UVs*, then select one of the UV's (any will do). In the UV texture editor menu, go to *Select>Select Shell*. This will select all UV's contiguously connected to

*Figure: 3.19*

the UV you selected. This tool will come in handy when trying to select only certain groups of UV's. Press "W" and move the UV's off to the side, out of the dark gray region, so we can have some room to work.

In the workspace, select all of the front faces of the tire as shown in Figure: 3.13. Go to *Create UV's>Planar Mapping* and select the options box. Make sure that *X Axis* is checked, and press the *Project* button. In the UV texture editor, you will see the front faces are projected from the front angle.

It is a good idea to separate the UV's along natural seams in the texture. One such seam is the area where the tire meets the metal rim of the wheel. Double-click to select the edge loop that would signify that split, as shown in Figure: 3.14. In the UV texture editor toolbar, click the sixth icon over which is the image with the pair of scissors. This breaks the shell of UV's along the selected edge. Now if you select the center UV in the front projection and go to *Select>Select Shell*, you can separate the metal part of the wheel away from the tire section.

Repeat the above process with the rear face of the tire as well. Now in the UV texture editor menu, go to *Polygons>Layout* and select the options box. Scroll down to the *Shell Spacing* section, and set *Percentage Space* to 1. Click *Layout UVs*. This will automatically re-size and re-arrange the UV shells.

 You have completed laying out the UV's for one of the four wheels. Luckily Maya gives you the ability to transfer these UV's to the other three wheels. First, select the wheel with the completed UV's, then select one of the unmapped wheels. Go to *Mesh>Transfer Attributes* and select the option box. Under *Attributes to Transfer*, set *Vertex Position* and *Vertex Normal* to off, and set *UV Sets* and *Color Sets* to *All*. Under *Attribute Settings*, set *Sample space* to *Topology*. Press the *Transfer* button. Now the second tire should also have the same UV layout. Repeat the process on the other two tires.

Now that the UV's are laid out for the wheel you can create a texture map. Select one of the wheels, and in the UV texture editor, go to *Polygons>UV Snapshot*. Change file name to *Wheel_UV*. Also change *Size X* and *Size Y* to 1024, and change *Image Format* to *PNG*. Press the *OK* button. Now you have a PNG image of your UV's in your *project>images* folder. You can take this file into the image editing software of your choice and use it as reference to create your texture map.

When dealing with a more complicated mesh, such as the cart base with no easily identifiable overall shape, the best option is to use automatic mapping as a starting point. Automatic mapping is essentially planar mapping from all 6 sides. The result is never perfect, but it will organize the UV's in a way that will help you see the next appropriate step. Select the cart base, and go to *Create UV's>Automatic Mapping*, and choose the options box. Under the *Optimize For* option, choose *Less distortion*. Click the *Project* button.

Select the faces along the side and front of the area under the seats and above the rear wheel well, and apply a cylindrical mapping to them. In the channel box, change the *Projection Horizontal Sweep* to 60. Move the newly projected section out of the way. Now if you wish to paint pin-striping or designs on this area, it is all one elongated canvas.

Select all the faces on the underside of the golf cart, and apply a planar map projecting from the Y axis. These faces will rarely be seen so they can be grouped together and textured together. A helpful selection tip is to select UV shells in the UV texture editor, then go to *Select>Convert Selection to Faces*.

Select the hood and side wheel wells, and again use cylindrical mapping on them. In the channel box, set the *Rotate X* value to -45 and the *Projection Horizontal Sweep* to 130.

What are left should be scattered pieces of the model. Determine which UV's represent specific parts of the model and manually organize them in an efficient way to allow yourself to create the texture map. You may come across sections that should be connected but are not. When this happens, move the shells as near to each other as possible, and align them as they should be. Use the sew UV button, directly below the separate UV button, to reconnect the edges.


UV mapping a model can be a long and tedious process, but it is essential to creating an appealing texture map for the mesh. Color and texture bring a vitality and life to the model by defining the surface quality. It is the shiny fresh coat of paint that makes the model distinctly yours.

# Chapter 4: Animation

If you dig through art history books, you might notice that many of the artists appeared to be preoccupied with the one thing drawing and painting simply cannot recreate: motion. Even many cave paintings were often an attempt to depict actions such as hunting. The last century and a half has brought aggressive advancements in the tools we use to recreate motion in our art. Now you have one of the world's most powerful animation tools, Maya, just a double-click away. So let's go make some stuff move.

Open a new scene and create a polygon sphere. Look at your time slider and make sure 1 is highlighted. This means you are on frame 1 of the animation. Select the sphere and Press the "S" key to set a keyframe. You will notice a vertical red line appears on the time slider at frame 1 to signify the keyframe. You will also notice in the channel box that all the channels on the sphere turned pink. This means that those channels contain keyframed animation. Click and drag the time slider until frame 12 is highlighted. Then, in the workspace, move, scale, and rotate the sphere randomly. With the sphere selected, you should press "S" again. Now drag the time slider back and forth between frames 1 and 12. You can see that Maya has created a transition using the two locations and shapes of the sphere.

To make animation in Maya one step easier, you can click the auto keyframe button (below the playback buttons-looks like a key). Set the time slider to frame 24, and move, rotate, and scale the object. You will notice a new red line on frame 24 where Maya automatically set a keyframe on the channels you moved. It is important to notice that not every channel on the object received a keyframe, only the channels that you edited.

Now at the end of your time slider, press the large play button (refer to Figure: 4.01). The animation will play through the three keyframes you have on the sphere. Most likely the animation is playing at the wrong speed. If you have a fast computer, it will be playing back very fast. Click the animation preferences button beside the auto keyframe button, and set *Playback speed* to *Real-time [24 fps]*.

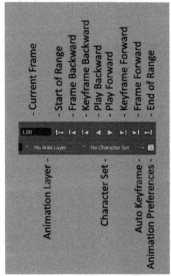

*Figure: 4.01*

Click *save* to close the animation preferences window. Now playback should be in real time.

The process of making objects move is very simple in Maya, as illustrated in the previous paragraphs. But we just covered a lot of information quickly. Let's look back and dig a little deeper into what you just did.

You may already be aware of how film and animation create the illusion of motion. Film is essentially a series of images displayed very quickly in succession. Each image is slightly different than the previous. Our minds automatically interpret the change in the images as motion. A television displays approximately 30 frames in a second, while a film projector displays the images at 24 frames a second. It is not an accident that Maya's range slider defaults to 24 frames, exactly one second of film animation.

A keyframe is a term coined by traditional pencil-and-paper animators. To plan out the action of the animation, traditional animators draw key points in the action to allow them to get the timing and poses correct. Once they have the keyframes, they can fill in the remaining frames to complete the animation. Filling in the "in-between" animations is known as tweening, and in traditional animation, it is often done by an assistant to the animator. Now Maya is your assistant.

Technically, in Maya, the keyframe is a marker in time on an object's attribute or channel. For example, on the first frame of an animation, you might set a key frame on the sphere's translate X value of 0. Then on the last frame you might set the translate X value at 100. Basically, you are telling Maya that at the first frame you want the value to be at 0, and at the last frame, you want the value to be at 100. These are markers on the values in time. With this data, Maya can draw a line between the two and determine what the translate X value should be at any frame in between them. Unfortunately, Maya is not the most intuitive assistant. Maya chooses the simplest route for this transition every time. Sometimes you want to be able to manually adjust the way Maya makes this transition. Select your sphere, and go to *Window>Animation Editors> Graph Editor*.

The graph editor is a visual representation of all the keyframes and their connecting curves for the object you have selected. Selecting individual channels in the graph editor's outliner isolates that specific channel's curve. Right to left on the graph represents time, counted in frame numbers. Up and down represents the channel value.

You can navigate in the graph view using the Alt + Right-click and Alt + Middle-click navigation options present in many of Maya's other editors and views.

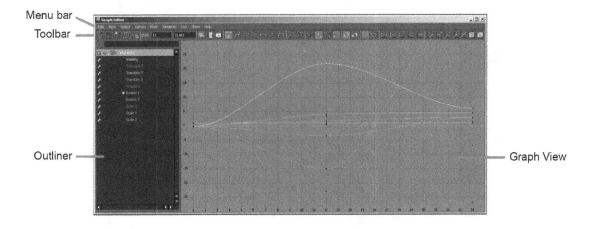

*Figure: 4.02*

If you marquee select one of the keyframes in the graph editor, you can move it with the middle mouse button. You will see that the selected keyframe has a handle that defines the tangent of the curve as it comes in and goes out of the keyframe. Marquee select one of the tangent handles. You can also use the middle mouse button to edit this tangent angle. This tangent handle will allow you to adjust the "ease in" and "ease out" of each key. By default, the tangents will be set to auto tangent mode. The

Figure: 4.03

buttons on the toolbar shown in Figure: 4.03 allow you to manually change each keyframe's tangent type.

The manual adjusting of curves and tangents is a crucial step in the animation process that newcomers often neglect. But it can make a drastic difference in the quality of the animation. The graph editor can be difficult to understand at first, but if you embrace it early, you will see that it is a very powerful animation tool.

## Rigging Basics

Rigging is the process of preparing an object for animation. You can model a wonderfully realistic human arm, but to Maya, it is just another mesh. Maya has no way of knowing where the arm should bend or how the skin should deform. You have to specify all of these things by setting up a rig for the arm before you can animate it. Rigging is an exercise in problem solving. It is a topic large enough for multiple books. Unfortunately, we can only scratch the surface here.

When considering how your models will move, the first thing to think about is the pivot point of the object. Create a polygon cube and rename it "UpperArm." In the channel box under INPUTS, change *Depth* to 4 on the *polyCube1* node. If you press the "E" key and rotate UpperArm, you will notice that the rotation is oriented around the center of the object. This is the default location for the pivot point, but you can change it. With UpperArm selected, press the insert key on your keyboard. The object's manipulator will change to a pivot point manipulator. It works exactly like the move manipulator. Select the translate Z (blue) axis handle, and move it to one end of the cube. If you hold X while

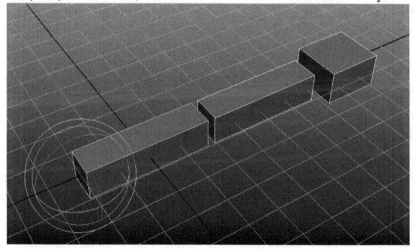

Figure: 4.05

moving the pivot manipulator, it will snap to the nearest grid point. The snap buttons can be found on

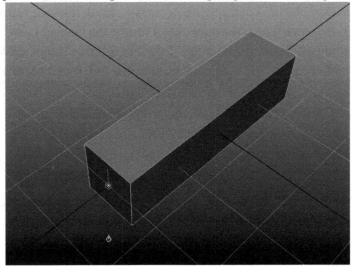

*Figure: 4.04*

the status line, and the shortcut keys are "X" for grid, "C" for curve, and "V" for point.

Press insert again to exit out of pivot point editing mode. Now UpperArm rotates from the new pivot point at one end of the cube.

The word hierarchy is often used to indicate a chain of command; the king outranks the prince, the president outranks the vice president, and the father outranks the son. In Maya, hierarchy is often called a parent-child relationship. To best understand this concept, open the outliner as you complete the next few steps.

Select UpperArm, and press Ctrl + D to duplicate the object. Rename the new object "Forearm." Duplicate Forearm and rename the new object "Hand." Move the hand and forearm to appropriate placements based on each name to create a full arm made of boxes. You can also scale the hand to more appropriately fit its name if you like.

You now have a very rudimentary example of an arm. But if you select UpperArm and rotate it, you will notice that the rest of the objects do not respond in the way an arm would. A real arm is an example of a simple hierarchy. If the upper arm moves, the forearm has no choice but to move with it. And if the forearm moves, the hand has no choice but to move with it. The upper arm is the parent to the forearm, and the forearm is the child of the upper arm. The child's movements do not affect the parent, but the parent's movements do affect the child.

To make the arm work correctly, we must first define the parent and child relationship between these three meshes. Select Forearm and then select UpperArm and press "P." The selection order is important in this process: child then parent.

If you select UpperArm in the workspace and rotate it, you will see that Forearm goes with it. If you rotate the Forearm, it does not affect the UpperArm. Press Ctrl + Z to undo the rotation.

You will notice two things have happened in the outliner. First, Forearm seems to have disappeared, and secondly, UpperArm now has a plus sign beside it. Click the plus sign, and you will see that Forearm is now under UpperArm.

The outliner is a very nice way to alter and interpret hierarchies in Maya because it closely resembles another familiar hierarchy system: a computer's file folder system. Because of this similar structure,

Figure: 4.06

you can also create a parent child relationship inside the outliner. Select Hand in the outliner, and middle mouse drag it onto Forearm. Now Hand is parented under Forearm.

Now you can rotate the objects in the workspace as if they were an arm. If you move Hand with the move tool and then rotate Forearm, Hand moves from its new position.

## Joints

Setting up a hierarchical system out of individual parts is fine for mechanical objects with separate pieces. But how are more organic objects rigged? A human arm is not three separate pieces; it is all one object. The answer is very similar to the way our arms really move, a skeletal system.

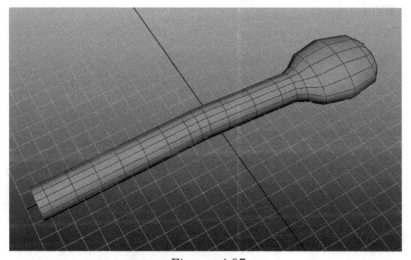

Figure: 4.07

To illustrate this, create a polygon cylinder, and quickly alter the edge loops to roughly resemble the shape of an arm, as shown in Figure: 4.07. Don't forget to put in a slight bend for the elbow.

Under the Animation menu set, select *Skeleton>Joint Tool*. In the workspace, you will notice that your mouse pointer has changed to a set of cross-hairs. In the top view, click at the base of the arm to create the first joint. Click and hold down the left mouse button again to place the second joint at the elbow. Holding down the shift key while creating this joint will lock the joint in a single axis. Create the remaining two joints, one at the wrist and one at the tip of the hand. Press enter to complete the joint creation.

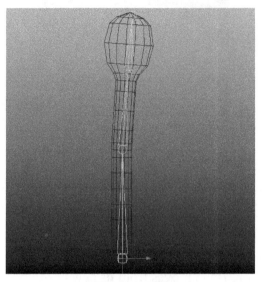

*Figure: 4.08*

If you open the outliner, you will see that the joints you just created exist in a similar hierarchy as the box arm we created in the previous section. Name the joints "UpperArm," "Forearm," "Hand," and "HandEnd."

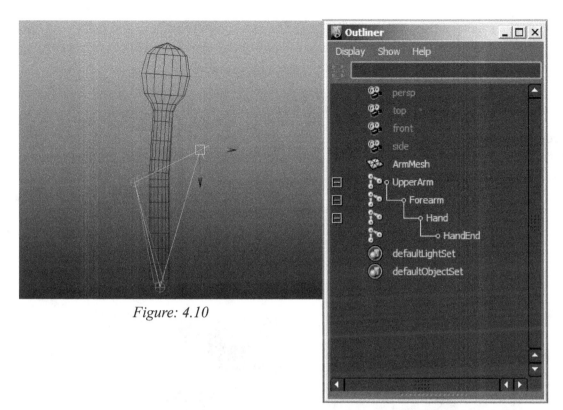

Figure: 4.10

Figure: 4.09

In the workspace, you can also rotate the joints down the hierarchy. This type of top down manipulation of a hierarchy is called forward kinematics or FK for short. But it is not the only way to manipulate a hierarchy. The alternative is inverse kinematics or IK. IK is a bottom up form of manipulation, meaning the hierarchical chain is controlled by an ending point.

Select *Skeleton>IK Handle Tool*. Again, your mouse pointer will become cross-hairs. Click on the UpperArm joint and then the Hand joint. The arm can now be controlled by IK. Select the IK handle, the small cross at the Hand joint, and move it around to see how IK affects the arm.

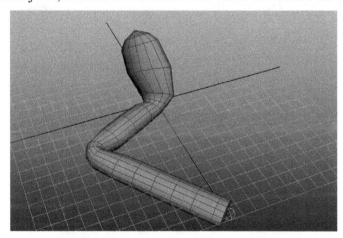

Figure: 4.11

Now you have a complete skeletal hierarchy that is controlled by either FK or IK. But it is still not making the arm model move. To achieve this, you have to tell Maya to apply the deformation of the joints to the mesh using a skin deformer. Select the UpperArm joint and the arm mesh, and click *Skin>Bind Skin> Smooth Bind*. Now if you edit the joints, the arm mesh will deform accordingly.

By default, the skinning on the mesh does a pretty good job, but it isn't perfect. Parts of the elbow are collapsing in on it and losing volume. To fix this, you can manually alter how the joints affect the mesh. Select the arm mesh, and go to *Skin>Edit Smooth Skin>Paint Skin Weight Tool*.

To effectively use the paint skin weights tool, you need to have tool settings open. Under influence, select the individual joints to see their influence on the mesh in the workspace. White means complete influence, and black means no influence at all. The red circle that appears when you mouse over the mesh is your brush for painting influence on the mesh. It uses the same painting system as the sculpt

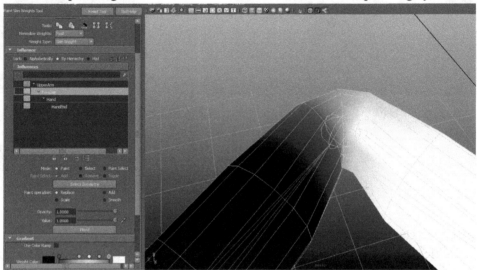

*Figure: 4.12*

geometry tool we used to create the ground mesh in the modeling chapter. In the tools settings under the influences list, you can change the value you are painting; 0 is black and 1 is white.

Painting skin weights can be tedious and difficult to predict. But the final result will pay off with an accurately deforming mesh ready for animation.

## The Bouncing Ball

The bouncing ball might seem like a tired, often overused example, but it rears its head so often for

*Figure: 4.13*

good reason. It is like learning the alphabet before learning to write sentences. In its simplicity, it contains the most important lessons that a newcomer to animation can learn.

Let's start with a new scene. Change the workspace layout using the fourth quick layout button from the top shown in Figure: 4.13. Change the top perspective camera view to an orthographic side view.

On each end of the range slider, set the playback range for 0 to 48 by changing the left and right most input boxes respectively. Turn on auto keyframe, and in the animation preferences, make sure the playback speed is set to real-time [24 fps].

Create a polygon sphere and rename it "Ball." In the channel box, set the Translate Y to 7 and the Translate Z to 9. Make sure the time slider is on frame 0, and press "S" to set a keyframe on all the channels.

Move the time slider to frame 12, and press "S" again to set a duplicate key.

On frame 6, set Translate Y to 1. Press "S" again just to set a keyframe on the channels that you did not edit. Now you have one complete bounce of the ball.

To add additional bounces, let's take a short cut. On frame 6 of the timeline, right click and choose *Copy*. Move the time slider to frame 18, and right click to choose *Paste>Paste*. Now you have a duplicate of frame 6 on frame 18.

You will notice that if you click drag along the time slider the animation of the ball plays back in the side view, updating in real time. Another way to steal a keyframe from the Maya time slider is to middle click drag. If you do this, the animation does not playback in the view. Middle click on frame 12, and drag the time slider to frame 24. With the ball selected, press the "S" key to set a keyframe thus creating a duplicate of frame 12. Scrub the time slider regularly to see the updated keyframe.

In the graph editor's outliner, select all the channels on the ball. On the graph editor toolbar, press the "frame all" button pictured in Figure: 4.14. Marquee select all the keyframes in the graph view, and

*Figure: 4.14*

press Ctrl + C to copy the selected keys. Move the time slider to frame 24, and press Ctrl + V to duplicate the copied keyframes.

If you press play on the playback buttons, you can watch the animation of the bouncing ball. But you might notice that the animation doesn't feel very bouncy. Instead, it feels more like a ball bobbing up and down in the water. This is why the tangents are needed.

In the graph editor, select the translate Y channel and the frame all button. This can also be done by pressing the "F" key. You will see that your curve resembles a sine wave with lots of ease in at the top and bottom of each peak and valley of the wave.

Remember that the translate Y channel is the up and down motion of the ball. The ease in and out at the top of the curve makes sense. As the ball travels upward, gravity affects the ball reducing the energy that launched the ball into the air in the first place. Eventually the gravity will overtake that energy, and the ball will slowly start falling back toward the ground. So the transition at the top of the ball's bounce should have lots of ease in and out, possibly even more than it has now.

However, the ease in and out at the bottom of each wave doesn't make sense when you consider how a ball really bounces. Imagine dropping a ball out of an airplane at 30,000 feet. The ball would fall faster and faster until it reaches a maximum speed called terminal velocity. The ball would have no idea that the ground is approaching, and even if it did, it would still be unable to slow down before it hits the ground. You can't control gravity. But the ease in and out at the bottom of each wave makes the ball slow down before it hits the ground.

The rebound of the ball as it bounces back up would also be very quick because bouncing off the ground is how the ball receives all of its energy. The ball should have its maximum energy and velocity when it leaves the ground on its travel upward. The ball would not ease out of its lowest keyframe, it would explode out of that keyframe with tremendous energy.

To achieve this, we will break the tangents at the bottom of each curve by selecting the keyframe at the bottom of the wave and pressing the break tangent button as shown in Figure: 4.15.

*Figure: 4.15*

Marquee select the left tangent, and move it up to break the in and out angle of the curve. You will see that this also increases the ease in and out on the keyframe at the top of the bounce. Repeat this process on all the impact key frames.

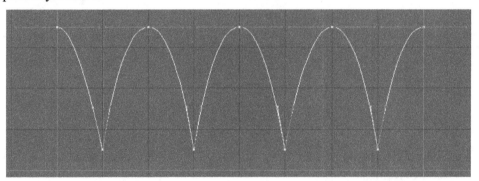

*Figure: 4.16*

Press the play button to see the animation. The bounce should now feel much more realistic.

Next, we are going to make the ball move forward in the Z axis, so the ball will feel like it is bouncing forward rather than in place. Select the translate Z channel in the graph. Select all the keyframes on the translate Z except the first and last, and press delete. Select the last keyframe on the Z channel.

At the top of the graph editor to the left of the tangent buttons are two number input boxes with the word *Stats* in front of them. This is the numerical data for the keyframe you have selected. The first number for the selected key is 48, the frame number of the keyframe. The second number is 9, the value of the channel. Change the value from 9 to -20, and press enter.

Now if you press play, you will see that the ball moves forward in the Z direction, but it starts the forward progression slowly. This is due to the ease out on the first key frame. To eliminate that ease out, select the first keyframe, and press the linear tangent button shown in Figure 4.17.

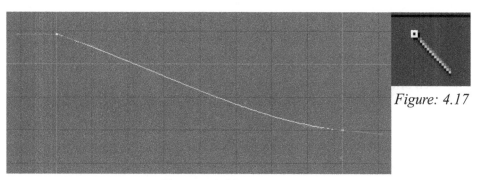

*Figure: 4.17*

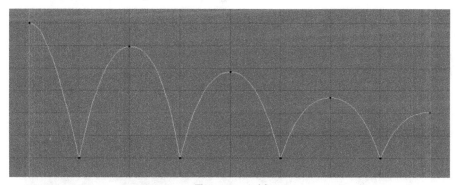

*Figure: 4.18*

The last keyframe on Z also eases in a little too much. We want some ease but not as much as it has now. Select the last keyframe on the Translate Z, and move the left tangent handle up slightly until it looks like the tangent in Figure: 4.18.

The same method can be used to add rotation to the ball. In the rotate X channel, delete all of the keyframes except the first and last. Select the last keyframe on the curve and change its value to - 500. Keep in mind the rotation channel's value is in degrees rather than units. This means the ball will rotate - 500 degrees. Select the first and last keyframe on the curve and set the tangent type to Linear.

In the real world, the ball would lose energy in each bounce resulting in smaller bounces. In the translate Y channel, you can manually reduce the height of each bounce by altering the keyframes at the top of each wave. This may require you to alter the tangents at the low point of the bounce again to ensure a nice ease in and out at the top of each bounce.

*Figure: 4.19*

Now, the animation looks much more like a real bouncing ball. But we can go even a step further and add a squashing and stretching effect to the ball. On the first frame of the animation, select the ball, and under the animation menu set, go to *Create Deformers>Nonlinear>Squash*.

In the INPUTS section of the graph editor, you can select *squash1* to see this deformer in action. If you enter 1 in the *Factor* channel, the ball will stretch. If you enter -1, it will squash. This is the value you will animate to get the squash and stretch.

But as you can see, the ball is squashing and stretching from its center. We want the squash and stretch to come from the bottom of the ball, where it contacts the ground. To do this, change the *squash1Handle*'s translate Y value to 6. This will lower the center of the squash deformer to the bottom of the ball. Now, on the *squash1* node, change the *Low Bound* to 0 and the *High Bound* to 2. Now if you change the factor, the ball appears to be squashing and stretching from the bottom.

Now, we have a squash deformer on the ball. If you scrub the time slider, you will see that the ball moves, but the squash deformer is left behind. We want the deformer to travel with the ball. We could parent it under the ball, but then the deformer would rotate along with the ball, and we always want the deformer to stay in the same orientation.

To achieve our desired effect, we will use a constraint. Select the ball, then select the squash deformer, and go to *Constrain>Point*. Select the options box. Check *Maintain offset*, and then click the *Add* button.

A constraint allows object A (in this case, the ball) to control the translation, rotation, and/or scale of object B (in this case, the squash deformer). A point constraint only effects the translate values of object B. So the squash deformer's location is controlled by the ball's location, but it is absolutely unaffected by the balls rotation. Note: all the translate values on the squash deformer are now light blue. This signifies that those channels are controlled by a constraint.

Now we can animate the *Factor* channel in the squash1 node. On frame 0, set factor to 0. Right click on the factor channel, and click *Key Selected* on the menu that expands. This sets a key only on the factor channel, as you can tell from the change of color in that channel. On frame 6, the impact point of the first bounce, set the factor value to -0.4. If auto keyframe is not on, you will have to right click on *Factor* and choose *Key Selected* again. On frame 5 and 7, the frames immediately before and after the impact, set factor to 0.4. On frame 12, set factor back to 0.

You can alter the angle of the rotation by animating the Rotate Z channel on the squash1Handle. It is helpful to have frames 5 and 7 stretching along the same angle the ball is traveling.

The ball is a normal round shape at the top of each bounce. At the impact frame of the bounce, the ball squashes. And in the frames before and after the squash, the ball stretches. This is to exaggerate the squash and the downward motion of the ball. Repeat this on all the bounces reducing the amount of squash and stretch as the bounces get smaller.

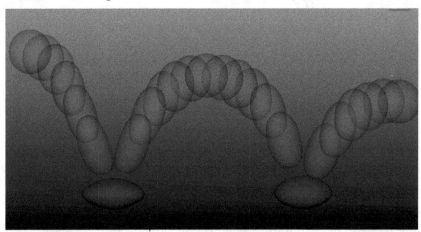

*Figure: 4.20*

To see a preview or playblast of this animation, you can go to *Window>Playblast*. Maya will create an avi video of the animation.


## *Rigging and Animating the Golf Cart.*

You have put a lot of work into making your golf cart model look great; now, let's make it move, too.

But first, we are going to have to do some setup to make animation easier. Open the latest version of the textured golf cart. For now, hide the ground mesh, so it doesn't get in the way.

First select a wheel. You will notice that the pivot point for the wheel is not in a sensible place for animation. A wheel would rotate from the center, so the ideal pivot point for this wheel would be the center. Rather than manually having to place the pivot, go to *Modify>Center Pivot*. Do this for each of the tires and the two axles. Also, center the pivot for each part of the steering system. Set the pivot for the foot pedals to the bottom of the pedal where it touches the floor.

In the outliner, make sure that all the pieces of the model are named correctly. If you still have nodes or data left over in the model's creation, delete them. Select all of the meshes, and delete the history, and freeze the transformation.

You may start to feel like the outliner is getting a little crowded and confusing, but remember the outliner works similarly to a file system on a computer. Select all the pieces of the golf cart model, and press Ctrl + G to group all the mesh into one node. This is like putting files in a folder. Note: the individual meshes still exist, they are now simply a child of a node called *group 1*. The group 1 node is like an invisible object. It has all of the standard translate, rotate, and scale channels, meaning its placement and size is both editable and animate-able. It also transforms all of the mesh with it. This makes it easier to move, rotate, and scale the entire model. Notice that the pivot point for the group is at the origin, which is exactly where we want it. Rename group 1 to "GolfCart_GRP."

The group is a nice way transform the entire model, but it does have one problem. It is invisible, making it hard to select. Let's create something that is easy to select and edit in the workspace. With interactive creation turned off, create a NURBS circle.

Under the INPUT node, change the circle's radius to 15. You do this resizing in the INPUT node, as opposed to using the scale channels, to keep scale set to 1. It is important to keep the values in the channel box as clean and simple as possible for animation purposes. When animating, it is always crucial to be able to get your channel box values back to their default setting, in case you need to start over on a section of animation. Being able to simply type 0 into translate and rotate and 1 into scale to get the model back to its default pose is vital.

Name the new NURBS circle "GolfCartMaster_CTRL." Be consistent in your naming conventions in case another person has to work on your rig later. The suffix GRP indicates a group and CTRL indicates an animation controller.

In the outliner, select *GolfCartMaster_CTRL* and then *GolfCart_GRP*. In the animation menu set, go to *Constrain>Scale* and then to *Constrain>Parent*. Now the *GolfCartMaster_CTRL* controls the entire model's translate, rotate, and scale. This is your master animation control for the golf cart.

Since the majority of the animation on the cart will be done on this controller, let's add some additional options to this controller to allow you to animate the wheels. Select the controller, and go to

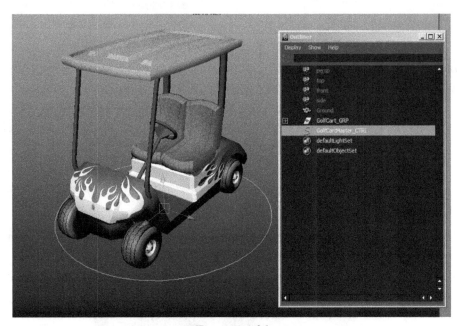

*Figure: 4.21*

*Figure: 4.22*

*Modify>Add Attribute.* The add attribute window will open. Under *Long Name*, enter "TireRoll." Make sure *Data Type* is set to *Float*, and press *OK*.

Now under the visibility channel, you have a new editable attribute called Tire Roll. But right now it doesn't do anything. We want this channel to manually rotate the tires forward and backward. Select the GolfCartMaster_CTRL, and go to *Window>General Editors>Connection Editor*.

The connection editor lets you directly connect attributes to each other, allowing one attribute's value to directly control another attribute's value. In the left column is the selected GolfCartMaster_CTRL attributes. If you scroll to the bottom of the list, you will find the newly created Tire Roll attribute. In the workspace, select the front left wheel, and in the connection editor, click the *Reload Right* button at the top of the window. Now in the right column, you will find all the attributes to the front left wheel. Between the *Reload Left* and *Reload Right* button is another button that says *From->To*. This button means that the attribute you select in the left column will directly control the attribute you select in the right column. In the left column, select the *Tire Roll* attribute. In the right column, select the *Rotate X* attribute. Close the connection editor. Now you will see that the tire roll channel directly affects the forward and backward rotation of the front left wheel. Repeat the process with the other three tires.

The connection editor is really good at making one to one connections, but sometimes you want a different result. This is where set driven keys come into play. Let's use a set driven key to create a wheel turn control for the front wheels.

On the GolfCartMaster_CTRL, create a new float attribute named "Wheel Turn," but this time under *Numeric Attribute Properties*, set the *Minimum* to -10, the *Maximum* to 10, and the default to 0.

Go to *Animate>Set Driven Key> Set*. Select the *GolfCartMaster_CTRL*, and in the *Set Driven Key* window, click the *Load Driver* button. Select the front left wheel, and click *Load Driven* button. On the GolfCartMaster_CTRL, select the wheel turn attribute, and on the wheel, select the rotate Y channel.

*Figure: 4.23*

Set driven keys allow you to define how the selected driver channel will affect the selected driven channel. Right now the wheel's rotate Y is set to 0 and so is the wheel turn attribute. This is a good place to start, so click the *Key* button. This means that now anytime the wheel turn attribute is set to 0 then the wheel's rotate Y axis will also be set to 0.

Now you can define the maximum value. When you created the attribute, you limited the maximum value to 10. But 10 degrees of rotation on the Y axis of the tire is not enough to make the turn feel realistic. Change the value of the wheel turn attribute to 10, and set the rotate Y value on the wheel to 50. In the set driven key window, click the key button again. By doing this, we have designated that when the wheel turn attribute is at 10, then the wheel's rotate Y channel will be at 50.

To set the minimum value key, change the wheel turn attribute to -10 and the rotate Y of the wheel to -50, and press the key button. Close the set driven key window.

*Figure: 4.24*

Now, adjusting the value of the wheel turn will cause the cart's wheel to rotate between its ideal minimum and maximum position. Repeat the process with the other front wheel.

The last thing we need to do is to make the steering system rotate with the wheels. Unfortunately, when modeling the objects, we had to reset the transformations on the steering objects. Now their rotation axis is not at an intuitive angle to achieve the correct steering rotation by simply changing a single rotation value.

To correct this issue, we are going to create a parent object for the entire steering system that is in the

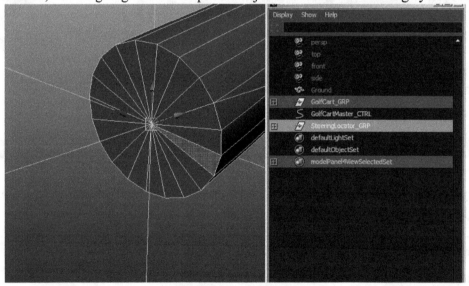

*Figure: 4.25*

correct orientation. Go to *Create>Locator*. A locator is an object that has a visual presence in the workspace but does not render. This is a nice helper node for situations just like this one.

To keep the rotation values at 0, select the locator, and press Ctrl + G to group it. Name the locator "SteeringLocator" and name the group "SteeringLocator_GRP." Now we can move the group to get the locator into the correct position and location while not affecting the channel values of the SteeringLocator.

In the outliner, select the SteeringLocator_GRP and the entire steering system. Next isolate the selection under the show panel menu. Select the SteeringLocator_GRP, and snap it to the center vertex of the steering column by holding "V" while moving it. Because the SteeringLocator_GRP is in the correct position so is its child, the SteeringLocator. But the values on the locator are still 0.

Getting the locator into the correct orientation is a little more difficult. In the sub-object face mode, select one of the cap faces on the end of the cylinder that makes up the steering column. Hold shift and select SteeringLocator_GRP. Go to *Constrain>Normal*. The orientation of the SteeringLocator_GRP now matches the direction the face's normal is pointing.

However, we do not want to keep this constraint, we only needed it to align the locator. To remove it, open the outliner, and delete the *SteeringLocator_GRP_normalConstraint1* node parented under the locator.

In the outliner, parent the SteeringLocator_GRP under the GolfCart_GRP, and parent all the steering mesh under the SteeringLocator. Now if you rotate the SteeringLocator in the Y axis, the steering system rotates with it.

Use a set driven key to connect the wheel turn attribute to the locator's rotate X axis. **Save the file.**

Now the golf cart is ready to animate, and the best part is that all the animate-able attributes are on one control, the GolfCartMaster_CTRL.

## *Making a Custom Button*

Sometimes, in the animation and rigging process, you will have to perform a task or series of tasks repeatedly. To alleviate some of the tedium, often these repetitive processes can be automated by creating a shelf button.

Open the script editor by going to *Window>General Editors>Script Editor*. The script editor can also be opened by clicking on the icon on the far right of the command line. This is the area where you can create, edit, and execute your own scripts in Maya using Python or Maya Embedded Language (MEL).

The bottom section is where you can input your scripts and the top section is where you can view the history of all the commands ran inside of Maya. Most likely it is filled with text. These are the commands for all the processes you had been preforming in Maya before you opened the script window. To clear these commands, you use *Edit>Clear History*.

With the script window open, select GolfCartMaster_CTRL in the workspace. In the history section of the script editor, you will see the following text appear:

*select -r GolfCartMaster_CTRL ;*

The command tells Maya to select something (**select**). It also says that if anything else is already selected, replace it with this new selection (**-r**). The command then lists the item to be selected (*GolfCartMaster_CTRL*). The command ends with a semicolon (**;**) to signify that the command is finished.

If you deselect the GolfCartMaster_CTRL, the following will print in the history window:

*select -cl ; .*

This is the command to clear all selections.

Every action in Maya has an associated MEL command. The history window is the easiest way to learn these commands. But even more importantly, it is where you can borrow these commands. For example, highlight *select -r GolfCartMaster_CTRL ;* in history, and use Ctrl + C to copy the text. Paste it into the input area, and press enter. The GolfCartMaster_CTRL will be selected in the workspace.

But suppose this control were difficult to select because of its positioning in the scene. You can create

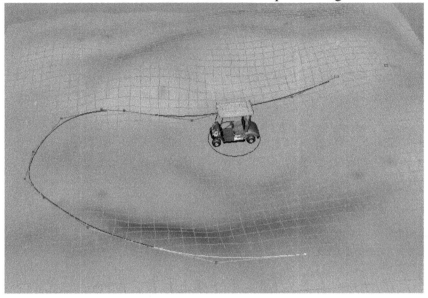

*Figure: 4.26*

a custom button that performs the action of selecting the control. Highlight *select -r GolfCartMaster_CTRL ;* , and middle mouse drag the text into the custom shelf. A window will pop up asking if you would like to save the script to the shelf as a MEL or Python. Choose MEL. Now you have a button in the shelf that will select GolfCartMaster_CTRL when clicked.

## *Animating the Golf Cart*

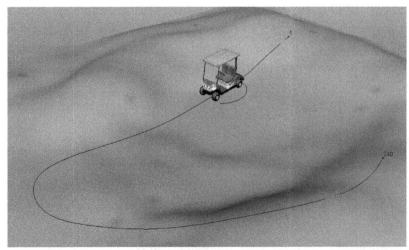

*Figure: 4.27*

Animating the golf cart across the sculpted ground plane could be a challenge using only keyframe animation. Maya has a tool that is perfect for assisting in this task.

First, set the range slider from 1 to 240 to give us approximately 10 seconds of animation time. Select the terrain, and go to *Modify>Make Live*. This means that items you move or create will now adhere to the surface of the ground mesh. Using the CV curve tool, draw a path along the surface of the ground mesh as shown in Figure: 4.26. When you are done, go back to *Modify>Make Not Live*.

Select the GolfCartMaster_CTRL and the newly created curve, and go to *Animate>Motion Paths>Attach to Motion Path*. Now if you scrub along the time slider, the cart will travel along the path. If the cart is upside down or sideways, correct this by altering the options under the *motionPath1* node. *Front Axis, Up Axis, Front Twist, Up Twist, and Side Twist* are all ways to adjust the orientation of the cart on the curve. In this case, by changing the front axis to Z, the issue will be fixed.

Alter the curve as needed to correct for tire penetration into the ground plane. If you need the cart to lean from side to side to accommodate for terrain, this can be achieved by animating the front twist attribute in the motionPath1 node.

Now all you need to do is keyframe the wheels to complete your animation of an unmanned, possibly haunted, golf cart wandering the putting green.

# Chapter 5: Lighting and Rendering

Rendering is where it all comes together. All of the hard work you have put into modeling and texturing your golf cart is all going to culminate in a shiny, new, beautiful render. But if you go to the status line and press the render button, you will most likely get something like the image found in Figure: 5.01.

*Figure: 5.01*

The model looks good, the texturing looks good, but the last crucial piece is lighting. Without it, no matter how much work you put into the rest of the project, the best you can hope for is a bland and lackluster result. The lighting you choose alters the mood and the entire emotional impact of the work. We are accustomed to lighting telling us about our environment. The lighting on this golf cart can determine if it is in a haunted forest, a forgotten garage, or a sunny golf course.

If you go to *Create>Lights*, you will see a list of the different lights available to you. These lights provide the different options to illuminating your scene. Each one of them works differently and will have a different effect on the way your model is rendered. Let's explore the different lights available to you and how they affect the objects in a scene.

The illustrations for this section were created by simply placing different lights inside an open-faced box with multicolored walls. All lights in Maya have an editable color and intensity setting. The default color of a light is white, and the default Intensity is 1.

A point light (Figure: 5.02) is one of the simplest lights you can create in Maya. Essentially it emanates light in all directions from a single point in space. A way to think of this light is a floating light-bulb casting light outward.

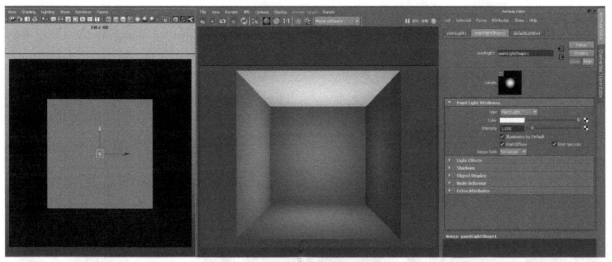

Figure: 5.02

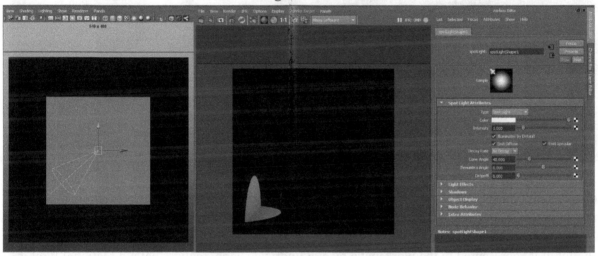

Figure: 5.03

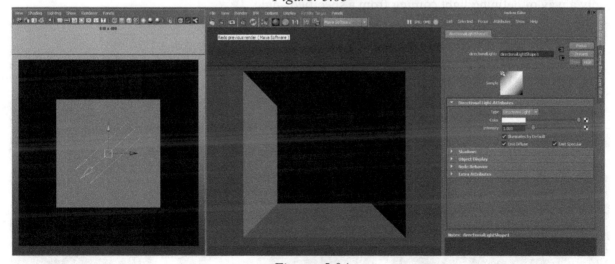

Figure: 5.04

A spot light (Figure: 5.03) is most easily associated with a flashlight. The light cast from a spot light radiates out in a single direction. The area affected by the light falls within a cone, as indicated from the light's shape. The size of the cone can be altered in the attribute editor by changing the *Cone Angle* value.

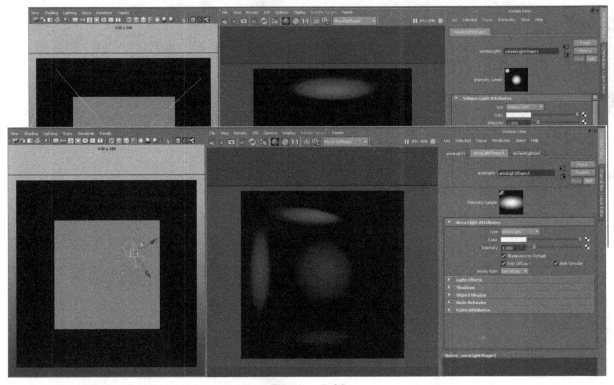

*Figure: 5.05*

A directional light (Figure: 5.04) is a harder light to explain because a real world example does not exist. In both the spot and point light, the source of the light is a single point. A directional light has no single point of origin. It is a light with infinite height and width casting in a single direction. Although it is represented in the workspace by a cylindrical shape, realize that a directional light is simply a way of defining light coming from a specified angle.

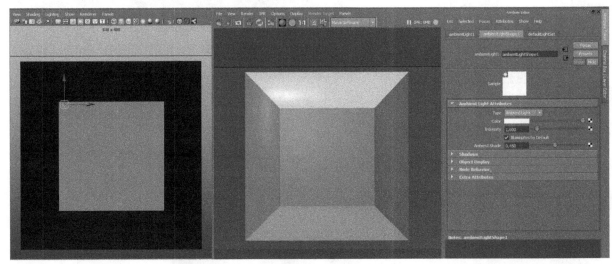

*Figure: 5.07*

An area light (Figure: 5.05) also has no single point of origin. Instead the light from an area light is cast from a rectangular 2D plane. This light is often softer and allows for more realistic shadowing, but is slower to render. A good real world example of an area light is a rectangular overhead florescent light. Like other lights, area lights have an intensity setting. However, the size of the light affects how much light is cast at that intensity. A large light has a large area and therefore casts more and brighter light.

A volume light (Figure: 5.06) is less like a light and more like a defined area of illumination. The shape is scalable and moveable, allowing you to specify the three-dimensional region that will be lit. Anything that falls within the light's space is illuminated.

An ambient light (Figure: 5.07) has two separate light sources. The first is the origin point of the light, which acts like a point light by casting light outward in all directions. The other is a light source emitting from all directions at one time as indicated by the name. The word ambient refers to the surrounding area, so think of an ambient light as a world light. It is a nice way to get overall base illumination for a scene.

## *Three Point Lighting*

Direct lighting is a term used when referring to lighting techniques that use the six lights we just discussed. Later in this chapter, we will explore indirect lighting methods as well. But for now, let's learn to use these lights to light your golf cart. We will do this by using a three point lighting setup. Three point lighting is a method used by many traditional photographers to illuminate a single subject or scene. The technique translates well into computer graphics and is often used by 3D artists to light their models in an appealing way.

After opening the golf cart file, we will create a render camera so you can tailor this lighting to a single view. Go to *Create>Cameras> Camera and Aim*. You have now created a new camera and an editable focal point. Hopefully, you are pretty familiar with navigating inside the view workspace. Instead of using the move and rotate tools to position this camera, use the navigation tools to place the camera in the view you prefer.

In the panel menu, select *Panels>Perspective>Camera1*. Now you are looking through the newly created camera. Track, dolly, and tumble the camera to compose a shot of the golf cart you would like for your render.

You might notice that the workspace is a slightly different shape than the output render you get when you press the quick render button. The size and shape of the final rendered image is based on the render settings that we will be exploring soon. But the workspace changes shape and size with the interface, making it hard to compose the shot accurately. Under the panel menu, turn on *View>Camera Settings>Resolution Gate*. Now the rendered region is indicated by a green line, allowing you to quickly visualize the area that will be visible in the final render. Frame the shot at an angle that clearly shows all the objects in an appealing composition.

If the resolution gate is not scaling appropriately with the panels, check on *View>Camera Settings> Overscan* from the panel menu.

To ensure you do not accidentally move the camera while you are working, we are going to lock the

*Figure: 5.09*

camera in place. Select *Camera1*, and in the channel box, highlight all the translate, rotate, and scale channels by click-dragging over their names. Right click, and choose *Lock Selected* from the menu.

Key Light

*Figure: 5.10*

Now all of the translate, rotate, and scale channels are locked, restricting the camera's movement and preventing you from accidentally ruining the composition.

This is also a good time to rename the camera to "RENDER."

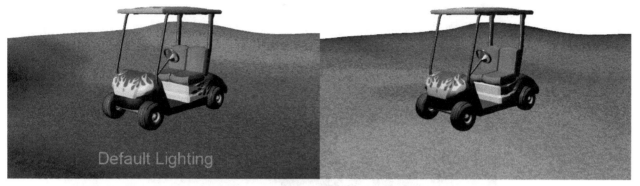

*Figure: 5.12*

*Figure: 5.11*

Change the panel layout to either *Two Panes Side by Side* or *Two Panes Stacked* depending on your preferences. Make one panel the RENDER camera and the other the persp camera. Now you can navigate freely in the persp camera and still see updates to the shot in the RENDER camera.

Press 7 in the RENDER camera to see the lighting in your scene. Most likely the view will simply show a dark silhouette of your scene, but as you start to add lights, you will see a preview of the lighting effects.

Press the quick render button in the status line to see the render of the scene with the default lighting. Click the green keep image button in the render view window, so you can refer back to the default render later.

By default, Maya has no lights in the scene, but to prevent all unlit scenes from simply rendering as black, Maya creates default scene illumination. When a direct light is created, the default scene lighting ceases to function. This is important to note because later in this chapter, we will explore ways of lighting the scene indirectly.

The first issue to address is the black background. No matter how many lights you place in the scene it will always seem like night if the background is dark. Select the RENDER camera by going to *View>Select Camera* on the panel menu. In the *Environment* tab, change the *Background Color* to white.

As the name alludes, the three point lighting setup contains three different lights. The first of these

*Figure: 5.13*

lights is a key light. This is the light that will provide the majority of the illumination on the object. Create a spot light, and name it "Key_Light."

As before with the camera, we could now manually move and rotate the light in position, but instead let's try another way of placing the light. Select the light, and in persp panel menus, go to *Panels>Look Through Selected*. The camera view has now changed to the perspective of the light, as if it were a camera. Now you can use the navigation options to position the light. Angle the camera to the left and slightly above the RENDER camera, pointing directly at the golf cart.

Press the render button in the render view to see the newly updated scene with the newly created key light. You will see a circle of light indicating where the cone angle stops. Adjust the *Cone Angle* in the spotlight settings until the light edge is outside of the visible render area.

Once you have a render where the cone's light edge is no longer visible, click the keep image button. Now you can drag the bar at the bottom of the render view to compare the differences between the default render and the render with the key light.

You will see that the default lighting that lit the entire scene is now gone. Now, the key light source is obviously coming from one side leaving other areas of the cart in darkness. But one particularly troubling element of the render is the fact that the golf cart now feels separated from the background, as if it is floating above the ground. That is because none of the objects in the scene are casting shadows, and the new key light makes this fact painfully obvious.

Shadows in the real world are the result of an object blocking a light source from another object. To calculate the way real light bounces around the world is an extremely time consuming and processor intensive way to render an image. Calculating the path of the light is called ray tracing, and although Maya's renderers can calculate ray tracing, it is important to consider the most efficient way to create the desired final render. Why use a very expensive process when there is an easier and faster way available? In the case of shadows, Maya gives you two options: Ray Tracing and Depth Map shadows.

Using depth map shadows is a quicker and simpler way to calculate shadows but at the expense of quality and accuracy. Depth map shadows analyze what is not visible from the perspective of the light and create an image of a shadow that is overlaid on the texture. The result is a quickly rendered shadow that requires only a small amount of calculation.

Select the Key_Light. In the attribute editor under the *Key_LightShape* node, expand the *Shadows* tab. Under *Depth Map Shadow Attributes*, check on *Use Depth Map Shadows*. Render the scene. As you can see, the light is now casting shadows.

Sometimes the depth map shadows can appear blocky and pixilated around the edges. *Resolution* is the second attribute under the depth map shadow attributes. As you can see, the resolution of the shadow map is currently set to 512. Just like any image, the higher the resolution the more fidelity in the image. Increasing this value will increase the quality of the shadow map, but it will also increase render time. Often a lighting artist's biggest challenge is balancing quality with efficiency.

For now, let's change the resolution value to 1024. Values in graphics are often represented by a power of 2 (32, 64, 128, 256, 512, 1024, 2048, 4096) for more efficient processing in a binary system. If you render the scene now, you will see that the resolution of the shadows is increased.

The *Filter Size* option increases the softness of the shadow. Be warned though that increasing this number will also increase render time dramatically. Set the filter size to 20, and render again. You will

*Figure: 5.14*

find that the shadows are nice and soft, but the render took longer.

The second type of shadows is called ray trace shadows. Under the *Depth Map Shadow Attributes*, you will find another tab labeled *Raytrace Shadow Attributes*. Under this tab, check on *Use Ray Trace Shadows*. Notice that the *Use Depth Map Shadows* option becomes unchecked. A light can only have one type of shadow at a time.

Render the scene. You will notice that the object no longer has shadows. The reason is because the render settings are currently not configured to do ray tracing. As mentioned earlier, ray tracing is a very computationally expensive process. By default, Maya's render settings are set to very basic options but allow you to turn on the more advanced options as you need them. This seems like a good time to explore the render settings window.

To open the render settings, click the last clapboard icon on the status line. It is the one with two dots beside it.

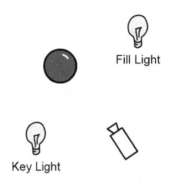

Fill Light

Key Light

*Figure: 5.15*

In the render settings window, you will notice two tabs. The first is labeled *Common* and the second is labeled *Maya Software*. The common tab is where you can specify the universal rendering options such as which frames to render in an animation, what file type to save, and where to save the files. It is also where you can determine the size of each render image. You can choose from some presets in the dropdown menu under the *Image Size* section. Choose the *HD 720* preset, so your future renders will be higher resolution.

*Figure: 5.16*

The common tab contains all the options that are consistent across all renderers. A renderer is a program that converts the data inside of Maya into a visible image by calculating light, faces, and textures. Maya's default renderer is called Maya Software. It is called this because software is doing the computational work to create each image.

A hardware renderer is a render option that utilizes the computer's graphics processor to render the

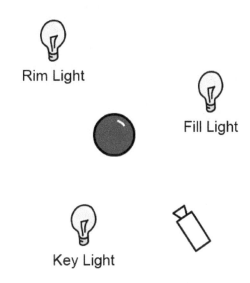

Rim Light

Fill Light

Key Light

*Figure: 5.17*

image. A video game engine is another example of a hardware renderer. The workspace camera view inside of Maya is also a hardware renderer. Hardware renders are often very fast, as proven by a game

*Figure: 5.18*

engine which renders video in real time. But that speed comes at a cost to quality. Software renderers take significantly longer but with that time come all the advanced and computationally expensive options that result in very high quality renders.

Maya Software renderer is capable of only direct lighting. Mental Ray, Render Man, and V Ray are third party software renderers that exist as alternatives to Maya's software renderer. We will explore Mental Ray later in this chapter, but for now, click on the Maya Software tab.

Under the *Anti-aliasing Quality* section, you will see a dropdown list labeled *quality*. This is a preset list for the anti-aliasing settings. Anti-aliasing smooths jagged pixels within a render. While setting up the lights, it is a good idea to leave this on *Preview quality* to allow for quick render times. But for the final renders, change this to *Production quality*.

Under the *Raytracing Quality* section, check on the raytracing button. Now if you render, you will see the raytrace shadows.

Back in the key light settings, we can explore the *Raytrace Shadow Attributes*. Unlike the depth map shadows, ray trace shadows only have three attributes. *Light Radius* is how you adjust the softness of the shadows. Raise the light radius to 2 and render the image.

The shadows are softer now, but the soft areas are very grainy. The reason for that is the second attribute, *Shadow Rays*. When rendering with raytrace shadows, the light object literally casts rays outward and measures where the rays bounce. The grainy shadows are the result of too few rays being cast. Upping the amount of shadow rays increases render time, so be careful with this number. Setting it to 10 should result in a pretty nice soft shadow.

Something else you might notice in the render with raytrace shadows is that your Blinn materials may

*Figure: 5.19*

be reflecting the environment around them. Reflections are created by a raytrace process. If necessary, take this time to adjust the reflectivity in the materials.

So now we have set up the key light; let's create the next light in the three point lighting setup. The second light is called a fill light. As the name indicates, the fill light is placed on the darker side of the object to fill in the dark areas left by the key light. This light is usually placed lower than the key light and the intensity is significantly less. For the fill light, create a point light and place it to the right of the camera at approximately the same height as the steering wheel.

Set the intensity of this light to 0.35, and change the color of the light to a pastel green to simulate the bounce light from the grass. The fill light's primary purpose is to fill in the dark areas on the object, so it is not necessary to have this light cast shadows.

Render the image to see the effects of the fill light. You will notice that areas such as the wheels and the side of the seats that were dark in previous renders are now illuminated.

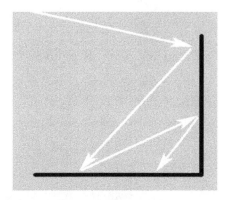

The final light in the three point lighting setup is the rim light. This light is to provide the rim highlight often used to outline product photographs. To achieve this, place a directional light on the opposite side of the golf cart as the camera.

*Figure: 5.21*

Change the color to a light pale blue to imply blue sky light and raise the intensity to 2. Uncheck *Emit Diffuse*. Now the light only affects the specularity of the object it hits, meaning it will cause Blinn and Anisotropic materials to have a strong blue highlight but will not raise the overall brightness of the object. Also, check *Use Depth Map Shadows*. This will block the light from parts of the model that are not in the uninterrupted path of the rim light.

Render the scene. The result of the rim light is subtle, but if you look at the top of the front passenger side tire or the top edge of the steering wheel, you will see a rim highlight outlining these areas of the model.

The scene is looking pretty good at this point, but the shadows from the key light are a little too dark to

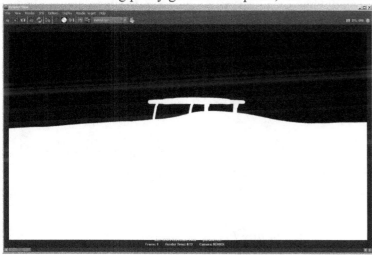

*Figure: 5.22*

for a daytime scene. To make the shadows less dark, change the shadow color on the key light to approximately 30% gray. Render the scene to see the result. **Save your progress.**

## Indirect Lighting

The three point lighting setup is only one of the lighting and rendering options available to you inside of Maya. Up to this point, all the lighting in the scene is the result of direct lights. Indirect lighting is lighting that comes from sources that are not one of the six lights Maya provides for you. Maya Software renderer is not capable of indirect lighting. So to explore indirect lighting, we will have to

*Figure: 5.23*

activate Mental Ray, one of the other renderers in Maya. Mental Ray is one of the most advanced rendering systems currently on the market and offers many powerful indirect lighting options.

Rather than continue with the previous three point lighting setup, let's relight the scene entirely using a different technique. Make sure you have saved your work, and then delete the three lights.

First we will need to change the renderer from Maya Software to Mental Ray. Mental Ray is a plug-in, and although it is supposed to automatically load when Maya opens, sometimes it fails to do so. In order to manually start the Mental Ray plug-in, you will need to click on *Window>Settings/ Preferences>Plug-in Manager*. Scroll down until you find *Mayatomr.mll* and check the *Loaded* and *Auto load* boxes. Close the plug-in manager.

Open the render settings. At the top of the render settings window in the *Render Using* drop-down box, choose Mental Ray. In addition to the common tab, you now have five additional tabs containing the Mental Ray render settings.

As we talked about earlier, when no lights are available, Maya uses default lighting to illuminate the scene. Since we are going to start lighting the scene with indirect lighting, we are going to disable the default lighting. Under the common tab in the render settings under *Render Option*s (all the way at the bottom), uncheck *Enable Default Light*.

Under the quality tab, you will find a dropdown box for *Quality Presets*. Choose *Preview:Final Gather*. Render the scene. The result will look similar to Figure: 5.19.

To reiterate, no lights are in this scene, yet the golf cart is illuminated and appears to be casting a shadow on the ground beneath it. Final gather is a way of simulating global illumination. Global illumination is lighting derived from other elements in the scene. In the above image, the lighting comes from the white environment color. The white of the environment casts light rays that bounce around the scene, illuminating the golf cart and ground. Select the camera, and change the environment color to a bright sky blue color. You will see that the color affects the overall lighting in the scene.

The reason the golf cart appears to be casting a shadow is because the light rays only bounce so many times before they fade away. Corners and tight spaces receive less ray bounces because of their obscured location. This is known as occlusion. The light is occluded from hard to reach areas, resulting in a shadow-like absence of light.

With final gather alone, the scene has a realistic, yet overcast feel to it. Think of final gather as base lighting. You can make the lighting even more appealing by adding direct lighting to emphasize specific areas. Let's create a directional light to imply the sun as a light source. In the channel box, change Translate Y to 30, Translate Z to 15, and Rotate X to -60. Change the light's color to a light yellow and the intensity to 0.5. Also, turn on raytrace shadows.

A combination of indirect and direct lighting can be used to quickly achieve very impressive results. Now additional fill and rim lights can be added to help emphasize specific areas of the model, if desired.

Although Maya's rendering capabilities are very powerful, often this is not the last step of the process. Once you have rendered the image you can take it into video or image editing software to combine it with other images and video clips in a process called compositing.

You are likely aware that digital image files on your computer are made up of three color channels: red, green, and blue (RGB). But some image formats such as .tga, .png, and .gif also contain an additional transparency channel known as an alpha channel. In the render view, if you click the icon with the circular checker pattern, you can view the render's alpha channel.

In an alpha channel, white signifies visible areas, while black is transparent. As you can see in this render, the blue background color of the render is transparent in the alpha. If you save the image as a .png and take it into a photo-editing program such as Photoshop, you can add a different background to the scene. It is important to note that compositing is not an afterthought in the rendering process. To achieve a well-composited image requires a lot of planning and resource gathering, as well as a skilled compositor and time. The illustration in Figure: 5.23 has none of that. It is simply intended to illustrate how alpha channels work.

## Non-Photorealistic Rendering

So far in this discussion of lighting and rendering, we have discussed processes focused primarily on realism or stylized realism. Indeed, that is the goal of most rendering software and processes. But photorealism is not your only rendering option. Luckily, Maya offers two standard non-photorealistic rendering alternatives.

The first is vector rendering. Like Mental Ray, sometimes the vector renderer does not automatically load when Maya starts, so it may require you to load the *VectorRender.mll* manually from the plug-in manager.

Because the final gather rendering method relies so heavily on Mental Ray's indirect lighting options, it would probably be best to start with an unlit version of the golf cart for this example. Once you have the file open and the vector plug-in loaded, go to the render settings, and under the *Render Using* drop-

*Figure: 5.24*
Render the image.

down box, choose *Maya Vector*.

The resulting render is made up of flat solid colors. The default setting essentially chooses an average color for each mesh and renders a vector trace of the object's shape. You can save this image as a raster image, but unlike other rendering methods, you can also save this render out as a vector image or even export sequences as .swf animations.

A lot of information is lost in this render, like details and shading. The result is a flatter, traditionally illustrated style. In the render settings under the *Maya Vector* tab, change the *Detail level preset* to *High*. This will increase the level of detail in each vector shape.

Add a second color to the render by choosing *Two color* fill style.

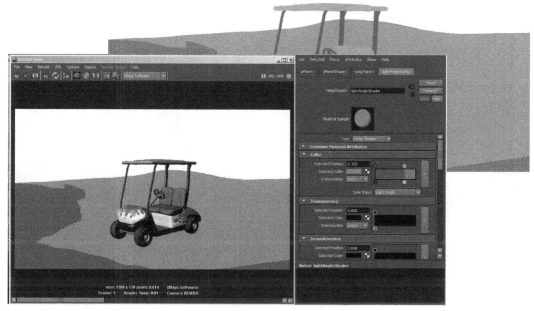

*Figure: 5.28*

*Figure: 5.25*

The result is interesting. You can start to see some of the detail in the wheels, roof, and seats. You can also see a very primitive interpretation of the flames on the cart's paint.

However, the scene is very dark. Let's add key and fill point lights to give the scene a little illumination. Set the key light's intensity to 1.4, and turn on its depth map shadows. Leave the fill light's intensity at 1.

In the render settings under the fill style, turn on shadows. This will add more depth to the shapes of the model. Also under *Edge Options*, check *Include edges* and set the *edge weight preset* to 0.5 pt. **Save** your work before rendering the image. It will probably take a while for the render to complete because of the number of calculations required to create the vector shapes. If the renders are taking too

*Figure: 5.30*

long on your computer, turn down the detail level preset.

*Figure: 5.26*

Although the vector render looks nice, the renders are time consuming and sometimes hard to control. Maya offers another option for cartoony rendering using Maya software renderer.

For this example, use an unlit scene of the golf cart. Start by selecting the ground mesh, and in the rendering menu set, go to *Toon>Assign Fill Shader>Solid Color*. The ground plane will turn white. If you look in the attribute editor, you will see that the ground mesh now has a new material called *solidShader.*

A shader is another word for material, although the word carries a larger meaning in certain contexts. Shaders are used to tell the GPU about specific rendering effects that are to be applied to the mesh. This new shader renders a single flat color across the entire surface without any shadows of gradation. The color is determined by the *Out Color* attribute. If you click on this color, you can change it to an earthy green to represent the grass.

Before rendering this image, you should open the render settings and change the renderer to Maya Software. Although Mental Ray can render the solidShader node, it cannot render other elements that we will later be applying to the scene. Render the scene, and you will see that the ground plane renders as a solid green color.

Although this solid color will be nice for some of the other cartoony elements in our scene, it might not be the best choice for the ground. It would be nice to have a second, darker color to indicate changes in elevation. So for the sake of experimentation, let's try another toon shader with more than one color option. Again, select the ground plane, and go to *Toon>Assign Fill Shader>Light Angle Two Tone.*

In the attribute editor, you will find the new *lightAngleShader.* By default, this shader has two color options. Select two earthy green colors with the left color being the darkest. You can also insert additional colors in the spectrum, but for now let's stick with two. Select the circle for the lightest shade of green, and change the *Selected Position* to 0.725.

Next, select the golf cart base, and apply a solid color shader to it by going to *Toon>Assign Fill Shader>Solid Color.* One of the benefits to using the Maya toon shaders over the vector render is the control over texture. So rather than having the base of the golf cart be a single flat color we can choose the texture image to apply to it. Click the checkerboard square at the end of the out color slider, and choose *File* from the create render node window that opens. In the attribute editor, point to the cart base texture file.

If you render the image now, you will see that the texture has been applied to the cart base but has no gradation or shading, giving the model a cartoonier feel. You can repeat this process with the seats and tires. But remember that if you used photographic images to texture your models then the effect might be somewhat unsettling. The texture maps for the render in Figure: 5.29 were digitally painted to keep with the illustrative, cartoony style of the render.

Also apply solid color shaders to the axils, pillars, bumpers, and steering system of the cart and change the out color to dark gray. Apply one last tan solid color shader to the roof. Render the scene.

The toon shaders are providing the scene with a very nice, illustrative quality, but one last element is missing to complete the style. Select all the objects in the scene, and go to *Toon>Assign Outline>Add New Toon Outline.*

In the workspace, you can now see that an outline surrounds the edges of the meshes. If you dolly around the scene in the persp camera, you will see that the lines change depending on the angle of the camera to the mesh. This outline is a Maya Paint Effects element that is applied post render to the scene. It is selectable in the workspace and very easy to manipulate in the attribute editor, as opposed to the lines in the vector render.

Select the outline, and in the attribute editor, change the *Line Width* to 0.18 to make the line thicker. Also change the *Line Ending Thinning* to 10. This causes the lines to taper to a point at the ends.

Currently the lines are only being rendered along the profile shape of the mesh. To add some detail lines inside the model's silhouette, scroll down in the attribute editor to the *Crease Line*s section. Change the *Crease Line Width* to 1.5. Turn *Crease Break Angle* to 180 and *Crease Angle Min* to 15. Uncheck *Hard Creases Only*.

**Save** the file and render the scene to see the results.


The final image of the toon render is hardly distinguishable as a three-dimensional object at all. Maya's lighting and rendering systems are versatile and capable of many different rendering styles and effects. In the hands of creative artists, these tools can be used to make countless stylistic decisions in the pursuit of unique artistic visions.

# Chapter 6: Effects

The word "effects" is often used as a blanket term to simply say "everything else." It is a catch-all category that is forever changing with the technology. Maya offers a robust group of effects tools and options that range from post-render lighting effects to dynamic physics simulations. To cover each facet of the effects possibilities would require volumes. This chapter will serve as your hors d'oeuvre tray to the world of effects in Maya; just a little sampler to give you a hint of the possibilities that await you.

The first thing you will notice is, under the *Menu set menu,* Maya has two different options: *Dynamics* and *nDynamics.* When you choose either of them, you will notice that many of the options sound similar. So what is going on here and what does that "N" stand for?

Maya has always had many dynamics options for particles and physics, but in version 8.5, Maya introduced nCloth which was a dynamic cloth simulation system driven by Nucleus. Nucleus is Autodesk's dynamic simulation framework that it plans to eventually implement into many other Autodesk products. After nCloth, nParticles followed, eventually allowing Nucleus the ability to drive almost all the dynamic simulations in Maya. Rather than eliminate the original dynamics system, Autodesk kept both. In other words, think of Dynamics as version 1.0 and nDynamics as version 2.0. They both do similar things, but for the purposes of this book, we are going to focus mainly on nDynamics because it is faster and more robust. However, it bears repeating that Maya's standard dynamics system is still a fully functional option that contains many tools similar to those in nDynamics.

Dynamic simulations are fun. It is very easy to start seeing impressive results within a few mouse clicks. Maya starts to seem like a physics playground. But don't be fooled, getting the perfect dynamics simulation is often the result of countless hours of work. And the best way to learn how to use them is to start playing.

Start by creating a polygon cube in a new scene. Open the outliner and rename the cube to "Box." Move the box up in the Y axis, approximately 10 units. Change the upper value of the range slider to 200. Now your time slider should show the range of 1 - 200.

With the box selected in the *nDynamics* menu set, chose *nMesh>Create nCloth.* To see the simulation, Maya has to start from the first frame. If you scrub the time slider, the box will move inconsistently and the right side of the command line will turn yellow, giving you the following error: *// **Warning: Nucleus evaluation skipped, frame change too large.*** The simulation must evaluate frame by frame, so move the time slider to the beginning of the animation. Press play to view the simulation.

If you are working on a slower computer, the simulations may start getting too complicated to play every frame at real time, causing the above error to come up again. It may become necessary for you to change the playback speed to *Play Every Frame.* If you do this, keep in mind you are not seeing the simulation at the accurate speed. You will need to playblast the animation to see it correctly.

The animation you are watching is somewhat lackluster, to say the least. It is simply a box falling downward in a straight line. But despite how un-dynamic this dynamic simulation is, it is important to notice what is happening. In the outliner, you will see two new objects in the scene. They are *nucleus1* and *nCloth1.*

*Figure: 6.01*

The nucleus1 object generates and calculates all the physics in the scene. By default in Maya, objects do not obey the laws of physics at all. When modeling, texturing, or even doing keyframe animation, the laws of physics aren't required. The nucleus1 object specifies that physics does exist in this scene and contains all of its settings for calculating the physics. It's the node that actually generates the physics.

The nCloth1 object specifies which objects will be affected by that physics and how the object will react. It is a sort of physics deformer on a mesh.

So let's make this simulation more interesting. Make sure you are on frame 1. Create a polygon plane and name it "Floor." In the floor's input under polyPlane1, change the width and height to 30. To make it a little more interesting, rotate the floor about 10 or 12 degrees in the Z axis.

Now with the floor selected, go to *nMesh>Create Passive Collider*. Press the play button to see the simulation.

Now the box is colliding with the floor and bouncing around and sliding down the slope. Feel free to experiment with different floor angles and different starting box angles. Each will result in a different simulation.

You will notice that now another new object exists inside the outliner called *nRigid1*. This node specifies that a designated mesh will collide and interact with simulated nucleus dynamic objects. It is interesting to note that the collider's position, rotation, and scale can be animated. Its motion is not simulated; it simply interacts with objects that are simulated.

Select the *nRigid1* object, and open the attribute editor. Under the *nRigidShape1* node, you will find the options that determine how the colliding mesh reacts. Under the *Collisions* tab, you will see the *Bounce* attribute. The higher this number the more objects will bounce when striking the collider. Set the number to something high, like 20, to see an exaggerated example of how bounce affects the colliding object. Friction determines how much resistance an object will encounter when sliding along the surface. Setting the friction to 0 makes the floor very slippery, like ice, while raising the number to 1 will cause the floor to react more like carpet or sand paper. The *Stickiness* attribute does exactly what it sounds like; it causes the colliding objects to stick to the floor. Raising the number to something high like 2 will cause the floor to react like flypaper. For now let's set bounce to 1, friction to 0.1, and stickiness to 0.

Now select the *nCloth1* object. In the attribute editor under the nClothShape1 node, you can alter how the mesh will deform. Under the collision tab, you will find similar options to those found in the nRigid1 object. These options are found here because other dynamic objects can also collide with the box.

Under the *Dynamic Properties* tab, you will find many of the options that will change how the mesh deforms. With a name like nCloth, you might not expect the box to react like a hard object. Fortunately, Maya takes the model's construction and volume into account when determining how it should deform. At this point, Maya is treating the box as if it is filled with air. If you lower the compression resistance to 0.3, you will see the box now reacts like a cube of gelatin rather than a rigid crate. But the box will not crush nor collapse, like a cardboard box, because it does not have enough polygons to cause that kind of deformation. Remember that an edge cannot bend; it is always a straight line. Even with low compression resistance, you can still make the object rigid by turning the rigidity to a high number, such as 10.

To make the box heavier, set the mass to 3. Now, you will see that the box falls a little faster and slides across the floor faster despite the friction settings.

Go to *Create>Polygon Primitives>Soccer Ball*, and move it up in the Y axis and over in the Z axis until it is near the same starting point as the box. Name it "Ball," and go to *nMesh>Create nCloth* to make the ball dynamic. In the Ball's *nClothShape2* node set, set the friction to 0.5 and mass to 2. Press play.

Now you have two objects falling and interacting with the floor. Let's continue to add additional dynamic objects. Create a polygon plane, name it "Curtain," and position it similarly to Figure: 6.02. Select the plane, and go to *nMesh>Create nCloth*. Press play to see the simulation.

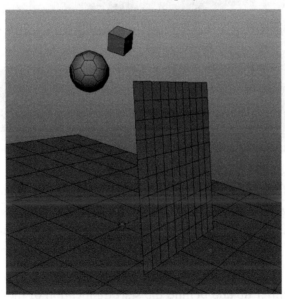

Figure: 6.02

You will see that the sheet collapses like a piece of fabric. Because the mesh is not enclosed, it does not react as if it is filled with air as the ball and box does. Let's make the curtain react more like its name by making it hang. Select the vertices along the top edge of the curtain mesh, and go to *nConstraint>Transform*.

Now if you press play, the top edge of vertices is pinned in space causing the remaining mesh to dangle

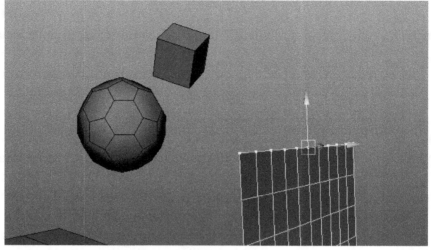

*Figure: 6.03*

like a curtain. The box and the ball collide with the curtain pushing it out of the way. To make the curtain deform more like thinner fabric, on the nClothShape node, set the thickness value to 0.01 and the stretch resistance to 1. Now, the cloth is more flexible. **Save the scene.**

One of the wonderful benefits of using nDynamics is the universal compatibility between effects that use Nucleus. Let's add dynamic particles to this scene to see what happens to our scene's objects.

*Figure: 6.04*

All particle effects consist of two elements: an emitter and the particles it emits. Go to *nParticles>Create nParticles>Create Emitter*. This will create both objects automatically at the origin of the scene. If you hit play, you will immediately see that the falling box and ball collide with the blue blobby particles.

Right now the particles are simply floating outward in all directions. Let's make them a little more interesting by moving the emitter up and behind the starting location of the ball and box. Use the outliner to select the emitter more easily.

With the *nParticle* object selected, select *Fields>Gravity*. Now the particles fall and interact with the rest of the scene.

Select the *nParticle1* object in the outliner. And in the attribute editor under the nParticleShape1 node, open the *Particle Size* tab, and change the radius to 0.7. This will make each individual particle larger. Under the *Radius Scale* tab, set the radius scale randomize to 0.4. Now the particles feel more like a heavy blue fog.

Under the *Shading* tab of the *nParticleShape,* you can change the physical appearance of the particles. Under the *Color* tab, you can change the blue color to a medium gray. You can even add additional shades of gray if you would like by clicking in the gradient area. Selecting the circle above the gradient allows you to move the location of that color on the gradient. Raise the input max to 5 and the

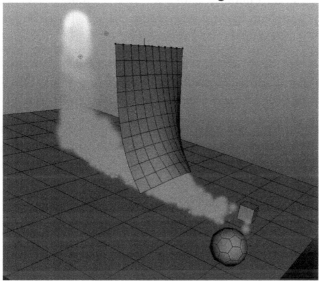

*Figure: 6.05*

color randomize to 0.3. Now the particles feel more like smoke.

Also, realize that you are not restricted to cloudy particles. At the top under the shading tab, you can change the particle render type to many different options. Blobby surfaces will allow you to create a more fluid style particle system, while sprites will allow you to apply individual images to each particle.

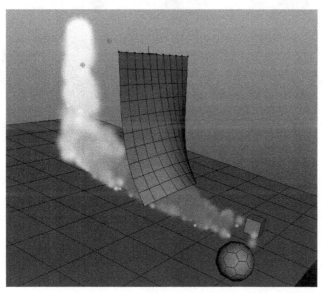

*Figure: 6.06*

The versatility of nParticles allows you to recreate substances as varied as fog, fire, smoke, explosions, and even liquid. The challenge for the particle effects artist is to recreate these substances by manipulating the particle's appearance and motion.

Effects are often used to recreate things that are too numerous to manually create or manipulate. The difficult process of replicating hair is always a challenging task. Maya offers two options for the creation of hair. They are hair and fur. Both hair and fur have their pros and cons to consider.

Fur, which can be found in the shelf under the fur tab, is a post-render effect on a mesh. The result is a beautifully rendered patch of soft fur, but it is not dynamic at all. It can be placed on dynamic objects, but it does not respect gravity or interact with other dynamic objects.

Hair, found under the dynamics menu set, is dynamic and responds to gravity and other objects. However, because each strand of hair is an actual dynamic object, it is often difficult to achieve a desirable render quality on hair.

Hair is also commonly used for rigging purposes. Due to hair's extreme dynamic flexibility, it offers many options for rigging objects that can be partially controlled and partially simulated like rope or a cord.

The real world is filled with things that can be difficult to replicate, even with an advanced software package such as Maya. Creative problem solving is often used to combine different effects elements to create the desired result. These are challenges effects artists face every day. Maya's robust effects

*Figure: 6.07*

package is an exciting toolbox at your disposal to solve the situations that arise daily in a production setting. Learning to use these tools creatively could be what sets you above the rest.

# Conclusion

Maya offers a hefty pallet of tools for the 3D artist to use in the creation of his or her craft. But with all its technological innovation and fancy bells and whistles, it is easy to forget that Maya is nothing more than a tool. Mastery of the tool is the job of the artist. Maya doesn't create exotic alien planets or loveable animated characters. Maya doesn't invent solutions to complex design problems or envision architectural marvels. On its own, Maya just sits on a hard drive and never creates a thing. It is you, the artist, who has to harness the power of this tool and use it. Tools were invented to make jobs easier. Your job, as an artist, is to create. Maya is your tool. Now go create something amazing.

# Glossary

**Animation** – The process of making objects appear to move by showing images of the objects with slight variations in quick succession.

**Bump Map** – A material option that is used to imply detailed depth information on a mesh. It is a similar process to normal mapping.

**Cartesian Coordinate System** – A mathematics concept that specifies a point in one, two, or three dimensional space (X,Y,Z).

**Depth Map Shadows** – A type of shadow that quickly calculates the area blocked by the light source and overlays the model with a mapping of the shadow area upon render.

**Direct Lighting** – The process of lighting a scene using the six light objects provided by Maya.

**Dolly** – The camera navigational option that allows you to physically move the camera closer or further away from the focal point. It is often mistaken for zooming. The shortcut key for dolly is Alt + Right Click.

**Global Illumination** – A form of indirect lighting that calculates the light bouncing and emanating from the other objects in the environment. Final gather is a form of global illumination.

**Hair and Fur** – The two systems Maya uses for the creation and rendering of individual hair follicles. Hair is dynamic but does not always have the best render quality. Fur renders beautifully but is not dynamic by default.

**Hardware Render** – Rendering that is done by the graphics processor. Hardware rendering is extremely fast but limited to less complex rendering features.

**Indirect Lighting** – The process of lighting with objects that are not Maya's lights. Global illumination and image based lighting are forms of indirect lighting.

**Keyframe** – A single frame in an animation that defines a distinct and important point usually is representing a pose. In Maya, it is a marker in time on an attribute's value.

**Lighting** – The process of setting up light sources to illuminate the models and set a mood.

**Material** – The node graph that tells Maya how to render the surface of a mesh.

**MEL** - Maya Embedded Language. The scripting language on which Maya is built. All the actions in Maya have a relating command in MEL.

**Mental Ray** – An extremely high quality software renderer that comes with Maya. Mental Ray offers advanced rendering options for indirect lighting.

**Modeling** – The process of creating and manipulating 3D geometry (like sculpting) to replicate real world or imagined objects in a virtual space.

**nDynamics** – The second generation dynamics system in Maya that utilizes Autodesk's cross-platform nucleus dynamics system.

**Node** – A single element of the computational data that makes up everything inside of Maya. Nodes are connected together to form more complex graphs. Behind every element in Maya is one of these complex node graphs.

**Normals** – The directional information that Maya uses to determine how light should interact with a polygon face.

**NURBS** – A type of 3D geometry that can be created inside of Maya. It is an acronym for Non-Uniform Rational B-Splines. A NURBS object has a smooth shape that can be altered by editing control points on the curves that define each NURBS surface.

**Polygons** – A type of 3D geometry that can be created inside of Maya. A polygon object is made up of individual points called vertices. Any two connected vertices make up an edge. Any enclosed areas of edges make a face. Vertices, edges, and faces are the editable sub-objects on a polygon object.

**Raytrace Shadows** – A shadow generation technique that casts rays from the light source in order to determine correct shadow placement. Raytrace shadows have higher quality and accuracy than depth map shadows but at the expense of longer render times.

**Rendering** – The process of combining the modeling, texturing, and lighting information into a final image.

**Software Render** – A type of rendering calculated by software. It is a slow way to render but provides extremely complex rendering options not often available in hardware rendering.

**Track** – The camera navigational option that moves your camera and the camera's focal point side to side and up and down. The shortcut key for track is Alt + Middle Click.

# Helpful Links and Resources

AREA (Autodesk's forum and help network)

http://area.autodesk.com/

Autodesk Education Community

http://students.autodesk.com/

Simply Maya (Maya learning community)

http://simplymaya.com/forum/

CGSociety (Forum and news)

http://forums.cgsociety.org/

3DTotal (Forum, news, and gallery)

http://www.3dtotal.com/

CG Hub (Forum, news, and gallery)

http://cghub.com/

CG Channel (Forums, news, and gallery)

http://www.cgchannel.com/

Game Artist Forum (Forum and news)

http://www.game-artist.net/forums/

3D Buzz (Forum and free tutorials)

http://www.3dbuzz.com/vbforum/sv_home.php

11 Second Club (Forum and monthly animation contest)

http://www.11secondclub.com/

Raph (Artist gallery and forum)

http://www.raph.com

Polycount (Forum, news, and gallery)

http://www.polycount.com/

Computer Graphics World (Magazine)

http://www.cgw.com/

Creative Crash (Plug-ins, rigs, and asset marketplace)

http://www.creativecrash.com/

Turbo Squid (Asset marketplace)

http://www.turbosquid.com/

CGTextures (Texture maps)

http://www.cgtextures.com/

Learning Maya (Tutorials)

http://www.learning-maya.com/

3D.sk (Human modeling reference images – requires paid subscription but has some free material)

http://www.3d.sk/

Environment Textures (Environment texture reference images – requires paid subscription but has some free material)

http://www.environment-textures.com/

Lynda (Video training for many types of software, including Maya)

http://www.lynda.com/

The Gnomon Workshop (Sells high quality training videos)

http://www.thegnomonworkshop.com/

Digital Tutors (Sells high quality training videos)

http://www.digitaltutors.com

You Tube (Search for user created Maya Tutorials.  Many are very good, and the best part is they are all free.)

http://www.youtube.com


Animation World Network (Animation news and articles)

http://www.awn.com/


Renderosity (Asset marketplace and gallery)

http://www.renderosity.com


3DM3 (Community and tutorials)

http://www.3dm3.com

www.ingramcontent.com/pod-product-compliance
Lightning Source LLC
Chambersburg PA
CBHW082111070326
40689CB00052B/4497